Nita Mehta's
Tempting
SNACKS

Including delicious snacks which are not fried

Nita Mehta

M.Sc. (Food & Nutrition), Gold Medalist

SNAB
Publishers Pvt Ltd

Nita Mehta's
Tempting
SNACKS

© Copyright 2001-2004 **SNAB** Publishers Pvt Ltd

4th Print 2004

ISBN 81-86004-94-7

Food Styling & Photography: **SNAB**

Layout and laser typesetting:

National Information Technology Academy
3A/3, Asaf Ali Road
New Delhi-110002
☎ 23252948

Published by:

SNAB
Publishers Pvt Ltd
3A/3 Asaf Ali Road
New Delhi-110002

Editorial and Marketing office:
E-159, Greater Kailash-II, N.Delhi-48
Tel: 91-11-23250091, 23252948, Fax: 29225218
Tel: 91-11-29214011, 29218727, 29218574
E-Mail: nitamehta@email.com
snab@snabindia.com

The Best of Cookery Books *Website:*http://www.nitamehta.com
Website: http://www.snabindia.com

Printed at:
THOMSON PRESS (INDIA) LIMITED

Distributed by:
THE VARIETY BOOK DEPOT
A.V.G. Bhavan, M 3 Con Circus
New Delhi - 110 001
Tel: 23417175, 23412567; Fax: 23415335

Price: Rs.189/-

INTRODUCTION

Snacks play a significant role while entertaining friends or family. This book will help you to prepare a variety of snacks to suit just about everyone's taste. The recipes that follow will smoothen the way to cooking for formal or informal gatherings, coffee parties, tea time parties or cocktails and will become long term family favourites.

I have arranged the snacks in such a manner, that it becomes easy for you to choose the right one. The unfried snacks are low in calories and can be offered daily without the dinner being disturbed. There are snacks which are a little heavy and thus may be relished at high tea parties. Cocktail snacks are given to serve as appetizers before a formal dinner. An interesting section on dips and chutneys to accompany the snacks is also included.

Remember, the most delicious food in the world can fail to tempt if it is presented in an unbecoming manner! A greasy or too oily snack is no more appetizing, so make it a habit to remove the fried snack from oil, on a tissue or paper napkin to absorb the excess oil. Always garnish your selected plate or platter but be careful not to make it too cluttered by over garnishing it. Often the best approach is to keep it simple. Fresh and crisp sprigs of mint, parsley, coriander, lettuce, onion rings go a long way. To make them look fresh at serving time keep these dipped in chilled water for 2-3 hours. Arrange them on the platter at the time of serving the snacks. Alongwith these greens, a red or a yellow rose made by rolling up a tomato or a lemon peel adds colour to the platter. If piercing a tooth pick in sandwiches, add an olive, grape or cherry to make it more attractive.

Happy Snacking!!

Nita Mehta

CONTENTS

TASTY SNACKS WITHOUT FRYING   9

ALL TIME FAMILY FAVOURITES   26

HIGH TEA SNACKS   47

SNACKS FROM AROUND THE WORLD   70

Tasty Snacks

WITHOUT FRYING

Whenever we think of preparing a snack, usually a fried one comes to our mind. Here I have listed some snacks which are tasty and yet not fried. They are either steamed, grilled or cooked in very small amount of oil or butter. These can be served as starters before a formal meal and even as tea time snacks. To serve as appetizers, keep the size small, usually bite size. Make them a little bigger when you want to serve them with tea or coffee.

Momos

A Tibetan snack, which can be steamed, baked or deep fried.

Makes 12   *Picture on facing page*

DOUGH
1 cup maida, 1 tbsp oil, ¼ tsp salt

FOR THE FILLING
2 tbsp oil, 1 onion - very finely chopped
1 tsp ginger garlic paste, 2 green chillies - finely chopped
4-5 mushrooms - chopped very finely (½ cup)
2 cups very finely chopped cabbage
1 carrot - very finely chopped or grated
1 tsp salt & ½ tsp pepper powder, or to taste, 1 tsp vinegar

RED HOT CHUTNEY
4-5 dry kashmiri red chillies - soaked in ¼ cup water
6-8 flakes garlic, 1 tsp saboot dhania, 1 tsp jeera, 1 tbsp oil
½ tsp salt, 1 tsp sugar
3 tbsp vinegar, ½ tsp soya sauce

1. Sift maida with salt. Add oil and knead with enough water to make a stiff dough of rolling consistency, as that for puries.
2. Heat oil in the kadhai for the filling. Add the chopped onion. Fry till it turns soft. Add the chopped green chillies and ginger-garlic paste. Mix well. Add mushrooms and cook further for 2 minutes. Add carrot and cabbage. Stir fry on high flame for 2-3 minutes. Add vinegar. Add salt, pepper to taste.
3. Make about 5 inch round puries of the maida, put 1 tbsp of the filling. Pick up the sides into loose folds like frills and keep collecting in the centre, to give a shape like that of a flattened ball (like kachorie).
4. Place the momos in a greased idli stand or steamer and steam it in a pan with a tight fitting lid with 2 cups water for 8-10 minutes. Remove from fire.
5. Remove each momo and place in a plate, keeping them spread out in the plate.
6. This momo can be had steamed, or it can be baked in the oven at 200°C for 7-8 minutes till light golden on the edges; or can be eaten after deep frying the steamed momos. Serve with chutney given below.
7. For the chutney, grind the soaked chillies along with the water, garlic, dhania, jeera, oil, salt and sugar and vinegar to a paste. Add soya sauce.

CHICKEN MOMOS

To make chicken momos, saute ½ cup and diced chicken instead of mushrooms. Stir fry for 4-5 minutes till cooked and then proceed further.

Spicy Mexican Triangles

Serves 6

6 slices of bread, butter - enough to spread

BEAN TOPPING
1/3 cup red rajmah (kidney beans) - soaked in 2 cups water overnight or for 5-6 hours
1 dry red chilli, 1 tbsp butter
½ tsp ajwain (carom seeds)
1 spring onion - finely chopped up to the greens
2 flakes garlic - finely chopped
1½ tbsp tomato ketchup, preferably masala or garlic flavoured hot tomato sauce
½ tsp salt, ¼ tsp pepper powder, ¼ tsp red chilli powder, or to taste

SPICY CREAM CHEESE
½ cup thick curd - hung for 15 minutes in a cloth
½ tsp salt, ¼ tsp freshly crushed pepper
1 green chilli - deseeded and very finely chopped

CRUNCHY GARNISH
2-3 tbsp chopped spring onion greens or coriander
2 tbsp roasted peanuts - crushed coarsely

1. To prepare the filling, pressure cook soaked rajmah along with ½ tsp salt, and dry, red chilli bits to give 2 whistles. Keep on low flame for 20 minutes after the second whistle. Keep aside.
2. Hang curd for 15 minutes. Beat well till smooth. Add salt and pepper to taste. Mix in very finely chopped green chillies. Keep cream cheese aside.
3. Heat butter. Add ajwain. Wait for a few seconds till golden.
4. Add garlic and fry till it starts to change colour.
5. Add the white part of the spring onion and stir fry till onion turns transparent.
6. Add rajmah along with the liquid, tomato sauce, salt and pepper. Cook till almost dry. Add some red chilli powder to taste. Remove from fire. Keep aside.
7. At serving time, toast bread slices till crisp. Butter them lightly and cut into 2 triangles.
8. Heat the rajmah topping. Put some hot rajmah on the toast, leaving the edges.
9. Put 2 tsp of cream cheese in the centre part.
10. Sprinkle some greens of the spring onion.
11. Put a few crushed peanuts. Serve immediately or heat in an oven at the time of serving.

Note: Tinned baked beans can be used instead of preparing the rajmah topping.

Haryali Murg Tikka

Serves 4

400 gm boneless chicken breast (boiler) - cut into 2" pieces (about 12 pieces)

1ST MARINADE
2 tbsp malt vinegar or lemon juice
¼ tsp salt

2ND MARINADE
200 gm spinach - discard stem and chop leaves
2 tbsp mint - chopped
2 tbsp green coriander - chopped
2 green chillies - chopped
1/3 cup hung curd (thick)
¼ cup thick cream
1 tbsp cornflour or besan
¼ tsp garam masala or tandoori masala, salt to taste

GARNISHING
lemon wedges
onion rings
chat masala to sprinkle

1. Wash and pat dry chicken pieces on a kitchen towel.
2. Marinate the pieces in vinegar and salt for ½ hour.
3. Discard the hard stems of spinach and chop. Wash it under running water.
4. Place the spinach in heavy bottomed pan. Cook on medium heat in its own water, stir till the spinach is little mushy. Cool. Squeeze out excess water.
5. Blend boiled spinach, mint, coriander and green chillies to a smooth green paste.
6. In a bowl mix spinach paste, curd, cream, cornflour, garam masala and salt.
7. Remove chicken pieces from the 1st marinade. Pat dry gently. Add to the spinach marinade. Marinate for 6-8 hours in the refrigerator.
8. Heat gas tandoor or oven to 200°C.
9. Skewer the tikkas or place them on grill rack. Roast for 8-10 minutes. Baste with oil or butter once in between. Cook till the pieces are tender.
10. Garnish with lemon wedges and onion rings and serve hot.

Keema Tarts

Makes 12-14

FILLING
250 gm keema (lamb or chicken mince)
1 large onion - chopped, 2 tomatoes - chopped
1 tsp ginger-garlic paste
3 tbsp oil
¼ tsp dhania powder (ground coriander) and ¼ tsp haldi (turmeric)
¼ tsp garam masala, salt and red chilli powder to taste

TART SHELLS
200 gm maida (plain flour), 100 gm white butter - well chilled (cold)
a big pinch of baking powder, a big pinch of salt

TOPPING
100 gm mozzarella or pizza cheese - grated
2 tbsp finely chopped capsicum or parsley or coriander

1. To prepare the filling, heat oil in a pressure cooker. Add onions and cook till light brown. Reduce heat and add ginger-garlic paste. Stir.
2. Add tomatoes. Cook till masala is well blended. Add salt, chilli powder, haldi, dhania and garam masala. Stir.
3. Add keema. Bhuno well till dry. Add 3/4 cup water and pressure cook lamb keema to give 2 whistles and keep on low heat for 3-4 minutes. For chicken keema, give 2 whistles and keep on low heat for 1-2 minutes only. Remove from heat.
4. After the pressure drops, bhuno the keema to dry the excess water.
5. When well fried, drain out the excess oil and keep the filling aside.
6. To prepare the tart shells, cut the cold, solid butter into small pieces.
7. To the maida add butter, baking powder and salt. Rub the butter into the maida with the finger tips till it resembles bread crumbs.
8. Add just 1-2 tbsp of ice cold water and knead into a dough of rolling consistency.
9. Roll out large, thin chappati of 1/8" thickness. Cut out small circles with a *steel katori* or biscuit cutter and fit them into tart shells.
10. Prick the shell with a fork and bake blind (empty tarts) at 230°C hot oven for 9 minutes. Remove the tarts from the shell. Cool and store in an air tight box.
11. To serve, spoon cooked keema in each tart. Top it with cheese and chopped capsicum or any green.
12. Again grill or bake at 210°C for 5 minutes, till the cheese melts. You can also do it in a microwave. Serve hot.

Chatpate Steamed Baby Corns

Serves 8-10

200 gm baby corns
2 tbsp rough coriander paste made by crushing a few coriander leaves
½ cup curd
1½ tsp garlic paste
2 green chillies - deseeded and chopped finely
1 tsp salt, or to taste, a pinch of haldi (turmeric)
some chaat masala - to sprinkle

1. Pressure cook all ingredients together, except the chaat masala, to give 1 whistle. Remove from fire. After the pressure drops, open the cooker and dry the water.
2. Serve sprinkled with some chaat masala.

Note: If baby corns are not available, cut the regular corn into 1½" pieces and pressure cook to give 1 whistle and then keep on low flame for 5 minutes. Choose tender corns.

Pan Crisp Paneer Sandwich

Makes 8

8 slices brown bread
butter - just enough to spread
some shredded carrot and cabbage, to garnish

FILLING
100 gm paneer - mashed roughly
1 capsicum - very finely diced
2 tsp tomato ketchup
2 green chillies - deseeded and chopped very finely
5-6 saboot kali mirch (pepper corns) - crushed roughly
salt to taste, 1 tsp softened butter

1. Mix all ingredients of the filling together. Add enough salt as it tastes bland otherwise.
2. Butter the slices. Spread a layer of the filling on the unbuttered side and press the second slice on it, keeping the buttered side out side.
3. Heat a non stick tawa or pan and put the sandwiches on it. Press with a potato masher to make them crisp. Turn sides to brown both sides.
4. Serve sprinkled with some shredded carrots and cabbage.

Spiced Button Idlis

Serves 8

Special saanchas (moulds) which make tiny (button) idlis are available these days. Enjoy these idlis without sambhar or chutney.

1 cup suji (semolina)
1½ cups curd, approx.
3/4 tsp Eno fruit salt
2 tbsp chopped hara dhania (fresh coriander)
3/4 tsp salt

TEMPERING (CHHOWNK)
2 tsp oil
1 tsp rai (small brown mustard seeds)
½ tsp red chilli flakes or chilli powder
7-8 saboot kali mirch (peppercorns) - coarsely crushed
a few curry leaves

1. Mix suji with curd to get a smooth batter of a soft dropping consistency. If the mixture is too thick, add some more curd.
2. Add Eno fruit salt, hara dhania and salt and mix well.
3. Immediately spoon the batter into the greased mould and steam for 14-15 minutes on medium flame till a knife inserted in it comes out clean. Cool and remove from mould and keep aside.
4. To temper the idlis, heat oil in a clean non stick kadhai or pan. Add rai and let it splutter for 1 minute. Remove from fire.
5. Add curry leaves. Add the idlis.
6. Sprinkle red chilli flakes and crushed peppercorns.
7. Return to fire. Mix well for 2-3 minutes. Serve hot.

Cucumber Chicken Sandwich

Serves 4

1 small chicken breast - boiled & shredded (½ cup)
½ cup hung curd or ½ cup mayonnaise
½ tsp lemon rind
¼ tsp saboot kali mirch (peppercorns) - crushed
½ tsp mustard and 1 tsp lemon juice
2 tbsp fresh or dried dill or mint
½ small cucumber - peeled and chopped very finely (½ cup)
6 slices white or brown bread

TO SERVE
a few black grapes or olives or cherries
2-3 lettuce leaves or mint or coriander sprigs - dipped in ice cold water for 2-3
hours
a firm tomato - peeled and rolled to form a rose
mustard sauce, a few tooth picks

1. To boil the chicken, place the chicken breast with ¼ cup water in a pressure cooker and a little salt and give 1 whistle. Remove from heat. Cool and shred the chicken into very small pieces.
2. To get ½ cup hung curd, hang 1 cup thick curd of full cream milk in a muslin cloth for about ½ hour. You may use mayonnaise instead.
3. To take out lemon rind, gently grate a whole lemon on a sharp grater very lightly, taking care not to grate the white pith below the yellow peel.
4. To the mayonnaise or hung curd, add shredded chicken, lemon rind, cucumber & dill or mint and mix well. Check seasonings, add pepper, mustard and salt if needed.
5. Spread the mixture generously on one slice of the bread, cover with another slice.
6. Repeat with the other slices to make 4 sandwiches. Trim the edges and cut diagonally.
7. Place the sandwiches on a platter. To garnish the sandwich, pass a toothpick through a grape, olive or cherry. Place a small piece of lettuce or a big leaf of mint in the middle of the sandwich and press the toothpick with the grape on it. Garnish the platter with a fresh lettuce or a coriander sprig and tomato roses made from tomato peels.

VARIATION
- You can use Avocados instead of cucumber. Cut the Avocados in half. Scoop out the pulp and mash. Add to the dressing.

Sesame Vegetable Coins

Makes 12

6 bread slices, preferably whole wheat (brown) bread
1½ tbsp oil
1 small onion - chopped finely
1 carrot - chopped finely (diced)
1 capsicum - chopped finely (diced)
2 small potatoes - boiled and grated
1 tbsp chopped coriander
1 tsp soya sauce, 1 tsp tomato sauce
½ tsp pepper, ¼ tsp chilli powder, salt to taste
sesame seeds (til) - to sprinkle
butter - just enough to spread lightly
2 tsp masala chilli sauce, or 1 tsp tomato ketchup mixed with 1 tsp chilli sauce - to serve

1. Heat 1½ tbsp oil. Add onions. Cook till transparent.
2. Add carrot and capsicum. Cook for 3-4 minutes on low flame.
3. Add potatoes, soya sauce, salt, pepper & chilli powder. Cook for 2-3 minutes. Keep aside.
4. With a cutter or a sharp lid, cut out small rounds (about 1½-2" diameter) of the bread. Butter the bread rounds very lightly on both sides with softened butter.
5. Heap some potato mixture on the round piece of bread in the centre, leaving ¼" empty all around, like a mountain. Press.
6. Sprinkle sesame seeds. Press.
7. Grill in a moderately hot oven at 200°C till bread turns crisp from the under side.
8. Serve, dotted with masala-chilli sauce.

Grilled Pancake Squares

Makes 16 pieces

PANCAKES
1 cup maida (plain flour)
2 eggs, 2 cups milk
¼ tsp baking powder, ¼ tsp salt

FILLING
3-4 cooked sausages or ham - chopped finely
½ cup cooked corn kernels
2-3 spring onions - chopped finely, 2 small capsicums - chopped finely
3-4 flakes garlic - chopped finely
8 tbsp cheese spread or grated cheese, 2 tbsp butter
mustard paste and pepper to taste

TOPPING
100 gm cheese (pizza or mozzarella) - grated
a few leaves of coriander or parsley

1. To prepare the pancakes, sift maida, salt and baking powder. Beat eggs in a bowl. Add milk. Add the sifted maida and beat well to a smooth batter. Keep aside.
2. Heat a small non stick pan. Grease it slightly. Remove the pan from fire and add a spoonful of batter. Immediately rotate the pan to spread the batter completely over the bottom of the pan. Cook on low or medium heat. Cook on one side only, do not flip to turn side, remove from heat. Keep the pancakes aside.
3. Save 1 tbsp of the batter for sealing the edges of the pancakes.
4. To prepare the filling, heat butter in the pan. Add spring onions and garlic. Stir. Add the capsicum, ham or sausages, corn, pepper and mustard paste and stir fry. Remove from heat. Keep filling aside.
5. To assemble the pancakes, place the pancake with the cooked side down on a flat surface. Spread a thin layer of cheese in the centre portion. Spoon a little filling on the cheese, fold all the four sides to get a small square or rectangle, of about 1½-2 inches. Stick the sides with a little left over batter of the pancakes.
6. To serve, grill the pancakes on a greased baking tray, keeping the tucked side down. Sprinkle 1 tbsp of grated cheese and coriander on each pancake.
7. Grill for 4-5 minutes, till the pancakes turn a little brown and the cheese melts.
8. Place pancakes on a bed of shredded lettuce or cabbage. Serve hot with the help of a flat spoon.

Note: If the frying pan is big, make big pancakes and cut them into half.

Minty Dal Kebabs

Serves 10

BOIL TOGETHER
1½ cups channe ki dal (split gram)
1 tsp salt, ½ tsp jeera (cumin seeds)
seeds of 1 moti illaichi (brown cardamom) - crushed
3-4 laung (cloves) - crushed
7-8 saboot kali mirch (peppercorns) - crushed
1" piece ginger - finely chopped
6-8 flakes garlic - finely chopped
2½ cups water

OTHER INGREDIENTS
3 slices bread
2 green chillies - chopped finely
2 onions - chopped finely
4-5 tbsp chopped poodina (mint)
½ tsp garam masala, ½ tsp amchoor (dried mango powder)

1. Clean, wash dal. Pressure cook dal with salt, jeera, crushed seeds of 1 moti illaichi, crushed laung, crushed saboot kali mirch, ginger, garlic and water.
2. After the first whistle, keep the cooker on slow fire for 15 minutes.
3. After the pressure drops down, mash the hot dal with a karchi. If there is any water, mash the dal on fire and dry the dal as well while you are mashing it. Remove from fire.
4. Soak bread slices in water for 1 second. Squeeze well to remove all the water.
5. Add squeezed bread, and all other ingredients to the mashed dal.
6. Add 1 tsp salt and ½ tsp red chilli powder to taste. Make small round discs.
7. Cook them on a nonstick tawa with just a tsp of oil till brown on both sides or grill at 230°C for about 20 minutes till done. After 5 minutes, brush with oil and turn sides. Grill till both sides turn brown. Serve hot with yogurt minty dip given on page 113.

Burgered Pizza with Mushrooms

Serves 8   *Picture on page 1*

8 mini pizza bases
250 gm chicken keema (mince)
½ onion - chopped finely
1 tsp ginger-garlic paste
1 slice bread - remove sides and crumble to get fresh crumbs
1 tsp worcestershire sauce
salt & pepper to taste

SAUCE
1 tbsp butter
3-4 mushrooms - sliced thinly
½ cup tomato puree, 1 tbsp tomato ketchup
½ tsp dried oregano
salt & red chilli powder to taste

TOPPING
50 gm mozzarella cheese - grated
½ capsicum - chopped finely

1. Grind the chicken mince in a mixer for a few seconds to get more binding in the chicken mince.
2. In a bowl, combine chicken mince, onion, ginger-garlic paste, fresh bread crumbs, sauce, salt and pepper. Mix well.
3. Form 8 flat tikkis of ¼" thickness, slightly smaller than the pizza base. Refrigerate for ½ hour.
4. Heat 2-3 tbsp oil in a non stick pan. Shallow fry the tikkis on both sides on medium heat. Keep aside.
5. To prepare the sauce, heat butter in a pan. Add mushrooms. Saute for 2 minutes. Add the tomato puree, ketchup, oregano, salt and chilli. Add ¼ cup of water and cook for 1 minute on low heat. Remove from heat.
6. Heat oven to 230°C. Oil the bottom and top of the pizza base slightly. Grill on a wire rack till the edges turn light brown and the under side of the base turns crisp.
7. Place tikki on the grilled pizza base. Top it with 2 tbsp of sauce.
8. Sprinkle grated cheese and chopped capsicum.
9. Place pizza on an oven tray and grill for 5 minutes or till cheese melts.
10. Serve hot with red chilli flakes and mustard sauce kept in small bowls.

Fish Tikka

Serves 6-8

500 gm boneless Singhara or Sole fish - cut into 2" cubes

1ST MARINADE
2 tbsp malt vinegar or lemon juice
¼ tsp red chilli powder
¼ tsp salt

2ND MARINADE
2 tbsp hung curd (hang 4 heaped tbsp curd to get 2 tbsp)
2 tbsp thick cream or malai
1 tsp ginger-garlic paste
½ tsp garam masala powder
½ tsp ajwain (carom seeds)
salt & chilli powder to taste

GARNISHING
lemon slices
mint or coriander sprig
some chat masala to sprinkle

1. Wash and pat dry the tikka pieces on a kitchen towel.
2. Marinate fish with lemon juice, salt and red chilli powder. Keep aside for ½ hour.
3. In a bowl mix curd, cream, ginger-garlic paste, garam masala, ajwain and little salt & chilli powder.
4. Add tikka pieces and coat well with this marinade. Keep aside for 3-4 hours.
5. Heat a gas tandoor on gas or an electric oven to 200°C.
6. Skewer tikkas or place them on the grill and roast till coating turns dry and golden brown. Baste with a little butter in between.
7. Serve hot garnished with lemon wedges and coriander. Sprinkle some chat masala.

Greek Meat Pockets

Serves 8   *Picture on page 1*

2 thick pizza bases
4 cooked sausages - thinly sliced diagonally
1 cup corn kernels (200 gm) - tinned
2 capsicums - sliced thinly
3-4 spring onions - sliced thinly
2-3 tbsp tomato puree
salt & pepper to taste
2 tbsp butter
some lettuce to garnish

TOPPING
1 tbsp butter
200 gm pizza cheese (mozzarella) - grated
1 tsp red chilli flakes
1 tsp dried oregano

1. Cut the pizza base into half. Slit open the cut side with the tip of a knife to make a deep pocket without damaging the top, bottom or sides of the base. Butter the top of the pizza and grill the base till slightly crisp.
2. Push a small lettuce leaf into the pocket if you wish. Keep aside.
3. Heat butter in a non stick pan. Add spring onions and capsicum. Saute for ½ minute. Add the sausages. Stir fry for a minute. Add the corn, tomato puree, pepper, pinch of salt and cook till puree dries and coats the mixture. Remove from heat.
4. Fill the pizza pockets with the mixture, carefully without damaging the base.
5. Slightly butter the top of the pizza and sprinkle grated cheese, chilli flakes and oregano on top of the pizza base.
6. Heat oven. Place the stuffed pizza on a greased tray. Grill (200-230°C) for 3-4 minutes till the cheese on top melts.
7. Cut each half in 2 pieces to get 4 pieces. You can cut them further into smaller pieces to serve with soups. Serve hot.

Chilli Paneer Footlongs

Serves 6

1 long loaf of French bread or garlic bread, some butter to spread
50-100 gm pizza cheese - grated
1 spring onion - chopped along with greens or ¼ capsicum and ¼ onion - diced
6-8 saboot kali mirch (peppercorns) - crushed
a few fresh red chillies - chopped, to garnish

TOMATO SPREAD
6-8 flakes garlic - crushed
¼ tsp red chilli powder
½ cup ready made tomato puree, 2 tbsp tomato sauce
1 tsp oregano (dried) or ½ tsp ajwain
salt and pepper to taste
1 tbsp oil

CHILLI PANEER TOPPING
100 gms paneer - cut into ¼" cubes
½ tbsp soya sauce, ½ tbsp vinegar
¼ tsp salt and ¼ tsp pepper, ½ tsp red chilli powder
½ tsp garlic paste

1. Marinate paneer cubes with soya sauce, vinegar, salt, pepper, chilli powder and garlic paste.
2. To prepare the spread, heat oil. Add garlic and cook till it just starts to change colour. Add all the other ingredients given under tomato spread and cook on low flame for 3-4 minutes till thick and oil separates. Keep aside.
3. To assemble, cut the loaf into two lengthwise. Butter each piece on the cut surface and the sides too.
4. Spread some tomato spread, sprinkle some grated cheese and then pick up the pieces of chilli paneer, leaving behind the marinade, and put on the loaf. Press gently.
5. Top with some spring onions or diced capsicum and onion. Sprinkle some more grated cheese. Sprinkle some crushed peppercorns and red chillies. Keep aside till serving time.
6. To serve, grill at 180°C for 8-10 minutes or till the loaf turns crisp. Cut into 2 inch pieces and serve.

Note: You may use boneless chicken breast (100 - 150 gms), boiled and cut into tiny pieces, instead of paneer to make chilli chicken foot longs.

Moong Dal Rolls

Serves 6

PANCAKES
1 cup moong dal (split green beans) - soaked for 1½ to 2 hours
2 tbsp coriander chopped very finely
3-4 green chillies - chopped very finely
½ tsp jeera (cumin seeds)
1 tsp salt, ½ tsp red chilli powder

FILLING
150-200 gms paneer (cottage cheese) - cut into 3-4" long thick fingers
2 tbsp oil
½ tsp salt, ½ tsp garam masala, ½ tsp tandoori masala, ½ tsp red chilli powder
1 capsicum - cut into half, deseeded and then cut into thin semi circles
1 onion - cut into half and then cut into thin semi circles
juice of ½ lemon
2-3 tbsp masala chilli tomato sauce

1. Soak dal for 1½-2 hours only. Strain. Grind with 1 cup water to a smooth batter. Add about ½ cup water to get a pouring consistency.
2. Add salt and chilli powder. Keep aside.
3. Prepare the paneer fingers by heating 2 tbsp oil in a non-stick pan. Reduce heat. Add ½ tsp salt, ½ tsp garam masala, ½ tsp tandoori masala and ½ tsp red chilli powder.
4. Add paneer pieces and mix gently with the oil. Saute for 1-2 minutes. Remove paneer from pan.
5. To the pan add the onion and capsicum strips. Mix well. Cook for 1-2 minutes. Sprinkle some lemon juice on them. Remove from pan and keep aside.
6. To prepare the pancake, wipe the pan with a paper napkin (tissue) and keep on fire. Smear 1 tsp oil in the centre and heat the pan but do not make it too hot.
7. Remove the pan off the fire and spread 1 karchhi (¼ cup) batter to make a pancake of about 5" diameter.
8. After a few seconds, pour some oil on the sides. Turn over when the under side is done, Cook the other side too. Turn again.
9. Spread some sauce on the pancake. Sprinkle some onion and capsicum strips.
10. Place the paneer piece at one end of the pancake. Roll it up. Keep the rolled pancake on the tawa for 2 minutes on low heat, pressing a little to heat the paneer inside. Serve hot.

All Time
FAMILY FAVOURITES

Enjoy these hearty snacks anytime and every time with family and friends. Perfect grilled sandwiches, crisp pizzas and delightful tikkas & kababs, which are all time favourites are included.

Amritsari Paneer

Serves 4

250 gms paneer - cut into thin fingers
2 tbsp ginger-garlic paste
½ tsp ajwain (carom seeds)
a few drops of orange colour
½ tsp each salt and red chilli powder
4-5 tbsp besan (gram flour)
oil for frying
chat masala to sprinkle

1. Mix ginger-garlic paste with ajwain, colour, salt and red chilli powder.
2. Marinate the paneer fingers with this paste till serving time.
3. At serving time, heat oil.
4. Sprinkle besan on the paneer fingers and mix gently to coat the paneer with besan.
5. Deep fry till crisp. Serve generously sprinkled with chaat masala.

Kalmi Kababs

Servings 15 pieces

1 cup channe ki dal (split gram) - soaked for 3 hours
2 green chillies - chopped finely
½" ginger piece - chopped finely
1 small potato - chopped finely
1 onion - chopped finely
2 tbsp finely chopped poodina (mint) leaves
3/4 tsp saboot kali mirch (pepper corns) - coarsely crushed
1 tsp salt
¼ tsp each - red chilli powder, garam masala & amchoor

1. Strain soaked dal. Grind dal with just a few tbsp of water to a coarse paste. Mix all other ingredients with the dal.
2. Add 1 tsp hot oil also to the paste. Beat well for 5 minutes.
3. Make 3 big balls. Flatten them so that they are ½" thick.
4. Deep fry to a light pink colour. Cool for 15-20 minutes.
5. At serving time, cut each kabab into 4-5 long pieces with a sharp knife.
6. Refry these long pieces to a golden brown colour. Serve hot with poodina chutney.

Pinwheels

Serves 4   *Picture on facing page*

6 slices of soft fresh bread
2 large potatoes - boiled and grated
1 onion - finely chopped
¼ cup finely chopped coriander
2 tbsp oil
½ tsp jeera
2 green chillies - deseeded & finely chopped
¼ tsp garam masala
¼ tsp haldi, 3/4 tsp salt, ¼ tsp chilli powder, ¼ tsp amchoor
1 tsp tomato ketchup

SEALING PASTE
2 tsp cornflour or maida mixed with 2 tbsp water to make a paste

1. Heat oil. Add jeera and cook till golden. Add green chillies and onions. Cook till onions turn transparent. Add salt, haldi, garam masala, red chilli powder and amchoor. Add the potatoes and coriander. Mix well. Add tomato ketchup. Keep filling aside.
2. Cut the sides of a slice, keep it flat on a rolling board.
3. Press, applying pressure with a rolling pin so that the holes of the bread close. Keep aside.
4. Similarly roll another slice.
5. Keep both the slices slightly overlapping at one end, about ¼" to get a long piece. Join the edges by applying some maida paste on the joint.
6. Spread a layer of the filling on the breads. Press the filling. Roll carefully.
7. Seal the end with maida paste.
8. Keep the roll, rolled up in a thin cloth for at least 10-15 minutes.
9. Deep fry each roll in hot oil till golden. Cut into 4 pieces and serve hot.

Note :   If you do not want fried pinwheels, apply softened butter on the roll and cut into 3 pieces. Bake in a greased oven proof glass dish for 5-10 minutes till light brown.

Fish 'n Chips

Serves 4-6

500 gm fish fillet (pomfret or sole) (8-10 pieces or fillet)

MARINADE
2 tsp lemon juice
salt, pepper to taste
1 tsp mustard powder, or to taste

BATTER
6-7 tbsp maida (plain flour)
2 egg yolks, 2 egg whites
6 tbsp milk or water
1 tbsp oil
a pinch of soda-bi-carbonate, 2 tbsp chopped coriander
salt & pepper to taste

COATING
1 cup fine white bread crumbs
oil for frying

TARTAR SAUCE - TO SERVE
½ cup mayonnaise
1 tbsp very finely chopped onion
1 tbsp chopped coriander or parsley
2 tbsp brown vinegar

1. Wash the fish fillet and pat dry on a kitchen towel.
2. Mix salt, pepper, mustard and lemon juice. Marinate fish with this mixture for 10-15 minutes.
3. Beat egg whites till stiff. Keep aside.
4. Make batter with maida, egg yolks, milk or water, oil, soda, salt & pepper. Fold in the egg whites.
5. Spread bread crumbs in a plate. Dip the fillet in the batter.
6. Roll in bread crumbs and fry on medium heat till golden brown.
7. To prepare the tartar sauce, soak the onion in vinegar for 10-15 minutes. Strain the onion to drain out the vinegar. Press gently to remove any excess vinegar. Gently mix it into the mayonnaise. Add the chopped parsley or coriander. Serve this sauce with fried fish.

Open Paneer Rolls

Makes 8 rolls   *Picture on page 119*

4 large potatoes - boiled & mashed very well or grated
3 tbsp cornflour
¾ tsp kala namak (rock salt)
a big pinch of haldi (turmeric)
3 tbsp chopped coriander
½ tsp salt, to taste, ½ tsp garam masala, ½ tsp amchoor, ½ tsp red chilli powder

FILLING
¾ cup grated paneer (cottage cheese)
½ capsicum - very finely chopped
1-2 tsp tomato sauce
2-3 green chillies - deseeded and chopped
¼ tsp red chilli powder, ¾ tsp salt, or to taste, ¼ tsp garam masala
3-4 almonds - chopped, 3-4 kishmish - chopped
oil for frying

1. Boil and mash potatoes very well while still hot or grate if they have turned cold.
2. Mix black salt, a pinch of haldi and pepper. Mix in the cornflour too. Add coriander, garam masala, amchoor, red chilli powder and salt to taste. Keep aside.
3. Grate paneer and add capsicum, tomato ketchup, green chillies, salt, red chilli powder, garam masala, almonds and kishmish.
4. Divide the potato mixture into 4 big balls.
5. With a ball of potato, make a 4" oval chappati on your hand, about 1/8" thick.
6. Place ¼ of the paneer on it and pick up the sides to cover the filling, such that the paneer is covered completely on all sides with the potato mixture. Shape to give a neat look with flattened ends.
7. Make all the rolls and keep aside.
8. Heat oil and deep fry till golden. These rolls can even be grilled.
9. Cut into two pieces lengthwise, exposing the paneer filling. Serve hot with a yogurt minty dip.

Paneer Tikka

Serves 4

300 gms paneer - cut into ½" thick, 1½" square pieces
1 capsicum - cut into fine rings
1 tomato - cut into long strips and pulp removed
2 onions - cut into fine rings
2 tbsp hung curd - (hang ¼ cup curd for 15 minutes)
1½" piece ginger
3-4 flakes garlic
2-3 dried, whole red chillies
½ tsp kala namak (rock salt)
½ tsp garam masala
¼ tsp jeera powder (cumin seeds)
a big pinch of haldi (turmeric powder)
1 tsp salt
juice of ½ lemon
4 tbsp oil

1. Cut paneer into 1½" squares, of ½" thickness.
2. Grind ginger, garlic and red chillies to a paste.
3. Mix curd, jeera powder, 2 tbsp oil, haldi, salt and kala namak to the paste.
4. Apply half of the paste on the paneer. Marinate at least for 2 hours.
5. At the time of serving, grill paneer pieces by arranging in a single layer in a greased oven proof dish in a hot oven till the paneer gets crisp from the sides.
6. In the meanwhile, heat 2 tbsp oil in a clean kadhai. Add capsicum and onion rings. Cook till onions turn pink.
7. Add the left over ginger-garlic paste. Mix well for ½ minute.
8. Add tomato strips, without pulp.
9. Add a few drops of lemon juice. Mix lightly.
10. Serve hot paneer surrounded by onions, capsicums and tomato strips. Sprinkle some lemon juice on the paneer also.

Classic Vegetarian Pizza

Serves 4-6

2 readymade pizza bases
100 - 150 gms mozarella or pizza cheese - grated

TOMATO SPREAD
2 tbsp oil
6-8 flakes of garlic - crushed to a paste
3/4 cup ready made tomato puree
2 tbsp tomato sauce
1 tsp oregano (dried), salt and pepper to taste

CLASSIC TOPPING
½ cup tinned sweet corn kernels
3-4 mushrooms - cut into paper thin slices
1 onion - cut into ½ and then into semi circles,
½ red and ½ green capsicum - cut into thin strips widthwise
a few black or green olives - sliced
1 firm tomato - cut into slices
salt and freshly ground peppercorns to taste

1. To prepare the tomato spread, heat oil. Add garlic. Stir and add tomato puree and tomato sauce, salt & pepper. Boil. Simmer for 3-4 minutes on low heat. Add oregano. Remove from heat.
2. Spread tomato spread on the pizza bases, leaving the edges clean. Sprinkle most of the cheese on the tomato spread (reserve a little for the top). Spread capsicum and onions. Sprinkle some salt and pepper. Sprinkle the mushrooms and corn. Arrange olives and slices of tomato. Sprinkle the remaining cheese. Sprinkle some oregano too.
3. Place the pizza on the wire rack of a hot oven (230°C). Grill till the base gets crsip and the cheese melts. To get a pan crisp pizza, oil the base a little before grilling.
4. Serve hot with chilli flakes and mustard sauce.

Afgani Murg Malai Tikka

Serves 4

400 gm (2-3 broiler) chicken breast (boneless) - cut into 2" pieces

1ST MARINADE
2 tbsp malt vinegar
2 tbsp ginger-garlic paste
salt to taste

2ND MARINADE
½ cup thick curd - hung for 15 minutes
¼ cup thick cream
2 cubes (40 gm) cheddar cheese (Britannia) - finely grated
1 egg
1 tbsp cornflour

1. Wash and pat dry the chicken pieces.
2. Marinate the pieces with the first marinade - salt, vinegar and ginger-garlic paste for ½ hour.
3. Mix cream, cheese, egg and cornflour to the curd.
4. Marinate the chicken pieces with this mixture for 2-3 hours in the refrigerator.
5. Heat an oven at 230°C or heat a gas tandoor for 15 minutes.
6. Thread the chicken pieces on skewers and grill them on the wire grill for 10-12 minutes, turning once in between and basting with oil or butter. Cook till tender.
7. Serve hot sprinkled with some chaat masala and lemon juice with chutney. Garnish with onion rings.

TANGRI KEBABS

You can make tangri kebabs in the same way. Take 8 drumsticks instead of boneless chicken.

Chicken Pakoras

Serves 4

½ kg boneless chicken - cut into 2" pieces
¼ cup (4 tbsp) thick curd
2 tsp ginger-garlic paste
salt & pepper to taste
some chaat masala to sprinkle

BATTER (BLEND TOGETHER IN A MIXER)
2 eggs
2 tbsp oil or 1 heaped tbsp salted butter
4 tbsp maida (plain flour)
salt & pepper to taste

1. Marinate the chicken pieces with curd, ginger-garlic paste, salt & pepper for ½ hour.
2. Heat 1 tsp oil in non stick pan. Add the chicken pieces and cook covered on low flame for 2-3 minutes till the chicken is tender and dry. Do not over cook the chicken, leave it succulent, because it will get cooked fully at the time of frying.
3. Blend all ingredients of the batter in a mixer.
4. Heat oil in kadhai. Dip individual pieces in batter and fry 3-4 pieces at a time on medium heat.
5. Remove from oil on paper napkins. Sprinkle chat masala. Serve with green chutney or tomato ketchup.

Keema Puff Pakora

Serves 4-6

250 gm lamb mince (keema)
4 tbsp maida (plain flour)
¼ tsp baking powder
3 eggs - beaten
2 green chillies - chopped
2 tbsp green coriander - chopped
1 tsp red chilli powder, ½ tsp haldi, salt to taste
oil for frying
chat masala to sprinkle
green coriander - to garnish

1. In a bowl, mix flour and baking powder. Add beaten eggs. Mix well. Add 1-2 tbsp of water. Beat well to get a smooth batter.
2. Add mince, green chillies, coriander, chilli powder, haldi and salt. Mix the mixture well. The mixture should have a soft dropping consistency. Set aside for atleast 1 hour or till frying time.
3. Heat oil on medium heat in a kadhai or a frying pan. Drop a few spoonfuls of batter at a time. Fry till crisp and brown.
4. Drain on paper napkins or any absorbent paper. Sprinkle chat masala and coriander. Serve hot with mint chutney.

Punjabi Aloo Tikki

Makes 10

½ kg (6 medium) potatoes - boiled and mashed
2 tbsp cornflour
1 tsp salt
ghee or oil for shallow frying

FILLING
1/3 cup channa dal (split Bengal gram)
½ tsp jeera (cumin seed)
½" piece ginger - finely chopped
2 green chillies - finely chopped
salt to taste
½ tsp red chilli powder
½ tsp chaat masala
½ garam masala
1 tbsp coriander leaves - chopped

1. Soak channe ki dal for 3-4 hours.
2. Heat 1 tbsp oil or ghee in a kadhai. Add jeera, wait till it turns golden. Add chopped ginger, green chillies, salt and red chilli powder.
3. Drain dal and add to the kadhai. Cover and let it cook on low heat till it turns soft and gets cooked. Sprinkle some water when it is being cooked.
4. Cook dal till soft and dry. Add chaat masala, garam masala and chopped coriander leaves. Remove from fire and keep aside to cool.
5. Boil, peel and mash potatoes. Add 2 tbsp cornflour and 1 tsp salt.
6. Take a ball of mashed potatoes. Oil the palm of the hand slightly. Make a shallow cup by making a depression with the thumb. Place 1 tbsp of dal filling in the depression and form a ball again to cover the filling. Flatten the ball.
7. Heat oil on a tawa or a frying pan. Shallow fry 2-3 tikkis at a time till well browned and crisp on both sides.
8. Serve hot with imli and poodina chutney.

Grilled Chicken Sandwiches

Serves 4-6   *Picture on facing page*

1 chicken breast - boiled and flaked
5-6 tbsp mayonnaise
½ onion - chopped very finely
8 bread slices, preferably brown
2 tbsp butter - to spread on slices

1. To boil the chicken, place the chicken breast with ¼ cup water and a little salt in a pressure cooker and give 1 whistle. Remove from heat. Cool and shred chicken into very small pieces.
2. Keep the shredded chicken and the chopped onion in a bowl and add enough mayonnaise to blend the chicken well with the mayonnaise.
3. Adjust seasonings of the filling by adding a dash of pepper, salt and mustard. Keep the seasonings of the filling a little strong because it may taste bland when spread on the bread.
4. Butter the bread slices on one side. Keep aside.
5. Spread the mixture on the unbuttered side of the bread slice and cover with another slice, keeping the buttered side outside. Repeat with other slices to make 4 sandwiches.
6. Heat your sandwich toaster or the oven to 220°C. Place the grill in the center of the oven. Place the sandwich on the grill or in the toaster and grill for 10 minutes or till the sandwiches are crisp and golden.
7. Cut into desired shape and serve hot with ketchup.

Note: When placed on the grill in the oven, press on the grill to get the lines or impressions on the sandwich.

Chicken Croquettes

Serves 6

1 hard boiled egg - chopped
½ cup boiled, cubed or shredded chicken
2 tbsp chopped green coriander
1 small onion - chopped
2 tbsp dry bread crumbs

WHITE SAUCE
2½ tbsp maida (flour)
2 tbsp butter
1 cup milk
salt & pepper to taste

COATING
1 egg - beaten
¾ cup dry bread crumbs

1. To boil the chicken, place the chicken breast with ¼ cup water and a little salt in a pressure cooker and give 1 whistle. Remove from heat. Cool and shred chicken into very small pieces.
2. To prepare the white sauce, heat butter in a heavy bottomed sauce pan or kadhai, add flour. Stir continuously on medium heat, until flour turns light brown.
3. Remove from heat and gradually add the milk, stirring continuously so as not to form lumps. If lumps do appear, press them against the sides of the utensil to dissolve them.
4. Put the sauce pan back on fire and cook till the white sauce turns very thick and starts leaving the sides of the pan. Add salt and pepper. Remove from heat.
5. Add to the white sauce - boiled and cubed chicken pieces, coriander, onion and 2 tbsp bread crumbs. Mix well. Gently mix in the chopped eggs. Cool the mixture, preferably refrigerate for a while, as it becomes easier to handle the mixture.
6. Shape the mixture into 12 rolls.
7. Dip each roll in beaten egg and coat well with bread crumbs.
8. Deep fry the croquettes on medium heat till golden brown.
9. Serve hot with tomato ketchup.

Bharwaan Paneer Pakore

Serves 4

250 gms paneer
some chaat masala to sprinkle

FILLING
½ tsp ajwain (carom seeds)
1 small onion - grated
1" ginger piece - grated and crushed to a paste
3-4 flakes garlic - crushed
½ tsp chilli powder, ½ tsp garam masala, ½ tsp salt
1½ tsp dhania powder (ground coriander)
1 tsp amchoor or powdered anaardana (pomegranate seeds)
1 tsp oil

BATTER
1 cup besan
1/3 cup water - approx.
2 pinches baking powder
3/4 tsp each red chilli powder and salt, or to taste
2 tbsp chopped coriander

1. Cut paneer into 1½" squares, keeping them slightly thicker than ¼ inch.
2. Sprinkle some chaat masala on them.
3. Slit the pieces of paneer, a little more than halfway but not till the end.
4. To prepare the filling, mix grated onion, crushed ginger and garlic. Add all other ingredients.
5. With the help of a knife insert some filling in the paneer pieces. Press well.
6. Prepare a thick batter with all the given ingredients. Beat well and keep aside for 10 minutes.
7. Dip the stuffed pieces of paneer in the batter and deep fry in hot oil till golden.
8. Serve hot sprinkled with chaat masala.

Spiced Chicken Cutlets

Serves 4-5

FILLING
250 gm (2 breasts)) boneless chicken - cut into tiny bits
¾ tsp kalonji (onion seeds)
½ tsp jeera (cumin seeds)
1 large onion - chopped, 2 green chillies - chopped
1 tbsp ginger - chopped, 1 tbsp garlic - chopped
2 red chillies (dried or fresh) - chopped
1 tbsp chopped mint, 2 tsp lemon juice
½ tsp coriander powder, salt to taste
3 tbsp oil

OUTER COVERING
4-5 large potatoes - boiled & mashed
1 tsp amchoor or chat masala, ½ tsp chilli powder, salt to taste

COATING
1 egg beaten with few drops of lemon & salt
¾ cup suji (semolina)
oil for shallow frying

1. To prepare the outer covering, mix mashed potatoes with amchoor or chat masala, salt & chilli powder. Keep aside.
2. To prepare the filling, heat oil. Add kalonji and jeera. When jeera turns golden, add chopped onion. Saute for ½ minute. Add chicken pieces. Stir fry for ½ minute and lower heat. Cook the chicken for about 3 minutes or till tender. Add garlic, ginger, red & green chillies, salt, coriander power, chopped mint and lemon juice. Mix well and remove from heat. Cool.
3. Make 8-10 balls of mashed potatoes. Flatten each ball on the palm of your hand.
4. Put 1-2 tbsp of filling in it. Wrap the potato mixture around the filling.
5. Flatten to make a cutlet.
6. Pinch the extra potato covering from the sides, to keep the potato wrapping thin. Similarly make 8-10 cutlets.
7. Heat oil in a shallow frying pan.
8. Spread suji in a plate.
9. Dip each cutlet in beaten egg, roll in suji and shallow fry on both sides till golden. Drain on absorbent paper.
10. Serve garnished with mint leaves and onion rings.

Club Sandwiches

Serves 4-6

2 chicken breasts - boiled and shredded
1 cup mayonnaise - recipe given below
9 large bread slices (of jumbo bread) - toasted and buttered lightly
3 lettuce leaf or a very thinly sliced cucumber (paper thin slices)
6 slices ham or bacon , 1 large tomato - cut into slices

1. To boil the chicken, place the chicken breast with ¼ cup water and a little salt in a pressure cooker and give 1 whistle. Remove from heat. Cool and shred chicken into very small pieces. Mix chicken with 2-3 tbsp mayonnaise and keep aside.
2. Place a lettuce leaf or cucumber slices on a toast. Top with chicken mayonnaise.
3. Cover with a slice, with the unbuttered side down. Spread some mayonnaise.
4. Place ham overlapping each other covering the whole slice.
5. Top with 2 tomato slices and cover with the last slice of bread with the buttered side down. To keep the filling intact while cutting, before cutting fasten the sandwich securely with wooden tooth picks. Pierce the tooth picks slightly away from the corners on all four sides.
6. Cut sandwich diagonally into 4 triangles. To garnish, pierce the tooth pick with an olive or a cherry. Place the sandwiches upright on a plate sprinkled with shredded lettuce.

MAYONNAISE
Gives 3/4 cup dressing

1 egg, ½ cup refined oil, ½ tsp mustard powder
1 tsp sugar, ¼ tsp salt, ¼ tsp pepper
1 tbsp vinegar or lemon juice

1. Add eggs, sugar & mustard to the blender of your mixer. Churn for 1-2 minutes.
2. Keeping the blender on, add oil slowly spoonful by spoonful, churning all the time.
3. Keep adding oil gradually, till it starts to thicken. Once the sauce thickens slightly, keeping the blender on, pour the oil in a thin stream from the cup directly in larger quantities. Churn till all the oil is used up & you get a thick mayonnaise dressing.
4. Add sugar, salt, pepper & vinegar. Churn once more. Remove from mixer to a bowl. Chill for 1-2 hours before use.

Note: If mayonnaise does not thicken or it curdles, remove from blender into a cup. Break another egg into the empty blender. Churn. Keeping the blender on, add the old mayonnaise from the cup, spoon by spoon, into the blender. Keep adding the old mayonnaise till all is used & a new perfect mayonnaise is ready.

Chicken Kaathi Rolls

Serves 6

A hot favourite at teenagers parties.

DOUGH FOR ROTIS
250 gm maida (plain flour)
2 potatoes - boiled and grated
1 tbsp oil
1 tsp salt or to taste

FILLING
500 gm boneless chicken - cut into small cubes
3 tbsp oil
1 large onion - ground to a paste
1 tbsp ginger-garlic paste
1 large tomato - chopped
1 tsp chilli powder, salt to taste
2 eggs - beaten
juice of 1 lemon
2 onions - thinly sliced & mixed with some hari chutney

1. To prepare the dough, sift maida. Add grated potato, oil and salt. Mix well. Knead into a firm dough of rolling consistency with some water. Cover and keep aside.
2. To prepare the filling, heat oil. Add onion paste and cook till light brown.
3. Add ginger-garlic paste and cook for 1 minute.
4. Add tomato and cook till tomato turns soft.
5. Add chicken. Cover and cook on low flame till chicken turns tender and dry. Remove from fire and keep aside.
6. Squeeze lemon juice to taste and add a pinch of salt & chilli powder.
7. Mix sliced onions with pudina chutney. Keep aside.
8. Beat eggs and add a pinch of salt and pepper. Keep aside.
9. To prepare the rotis, make thin chapatis out of the prepared dough by cooking the rotis lightly on both sides on the tawa. Keep the cooked rotis in a casserole.
10. At serving time, heat tawa. Add 1 tsp of oil and fry the chapati on one side only. Do not turn.
11. Pour 2 tbsp of beaten egg on the chapati and flip (turn) the roti to cook the egg. Remove from tawa, keeping the egg coated side up.
12. Sprinkle 1 tsp lemon juice on the egg coated side of the roti.

contd......

13. Arrange chicken filling on one end of the roti. Sprinkle some onions on the chicken filling and roll the roti forward tightly to form the Kaathi Roti.
14. To serve wrap the lower part of the rotis in a paper napkin.

Note: Ideal for teenage parties, as it can be prepared well in advance and heated for a few seconds in a microwave along with the napkin.

For mutton filling, substitute chicken with mutton. Prepare the mutton filling in a pressure cooker to make the mutton tender.

Crunchy Egg Sandwich

Serves 4

8 slices bread
2 eggs - hard boiled
1 heaped tbsp softened, salted butter
1 cube cheese - grated
½ tsp pepper powder, ½ tsp mustard powder
1 small capsicum - deseeded and very finely chopped

1. Mash the boiled eggs finely with a fork.
2. Add soft butter, cheese, seasoning and capsicum. Mix well to form a spread. Add a little salt after tasting the spread.
3. Spread this egg spread well on to a slice and top it with another slice. Cut into two triangles.
4. Store them in damp cloth till serving. Cut sides and serve soft.

Note: This spread can be prepared well in advance.

Toasted bread cut into small rounds and spread with this egg spread makes a delicious cocktail snack.

Chilli Chicken Pizza

Serves 4-6

2 readymade pizza bases
100 - 150 gms pizza cheese - grated

TOMATO SPREAD
2 tbsp oil
¼ tsp red chilli paste or red chilli powder
3/4 cup ready made tomato puree, 2 tbsp tomato sauce
1 tsp oregano (dried), salt and pepper to taste

CHILLI CHICKEN TOPPING
1 boneless chicken breast (100 - 150 gms) cut into ½" pieces
¼ tsp red chilli paste or powder, 1 tsp soya sauce
a pinch of ajinomoto (optional), salt & pepper
1-2 tbsp cornflour/maida
oil for frying
1 small onion - chopped
1 small capsicum - chopped

1 To prepare the tomato spread, heat oil on medium heat in a non stick pan. Add garlic. Stir and add chilli paste or powder, tomato puree, tomato sauce, salt & pepper. Simmer for 3-4 minutes till oil separates. Add oregano. Mix well. Remove from heat.

2. To prepare the chilli chicken topping, cut the chicken breast into ½" bit pieces. In a bowl marinate chicken pieces with chilli paste, soya sauce, salt, pepper and ajinomoto for ½ hour.

3. Heat oil in a kadhai. Drain the extra marinade from chicken pieces. Sprinkle flour and mix well to coat. Fry chicken on medium heat till crisp and light brown. Drain from oil.

4. Mix 1 tbsp of the prepared tomato spread with the chicken pieces to keep the chicken succulent and not turn too dry while grilling.

5. To assemble the pizza, spread tomato spread on the pizza base. Sprinkle most of the cheese on the tomato spread (reserve a little for the top). Spread chilli chicken, chopped capsicum and onions. Sprinkle the remaining cheese.

6. Place the pizza on the wire rack of a hot oven (300°F). Grill till the base gets crsip (to get a pan (crisp) pizza, oil the base a little before grilling.)

7. Serve hot with chilli flakes and mustard sauce.

HIGH TEA

Snacks

Delicious snacks which are filling enough to take the place for dinner. They make good TV meals too.

Baby Corn & Mushroom Quiche

Serves 4   *Picture on facing page*

SHELL
1/3 cup melted butter, 1½ cups maida (plain flour)
a big pinch of baking powder
¼ cup grated cheese, 3 tbsp water, or as required

FILLING
3/4 cup sliced baby corns - blanched with a pinch of haldi for colour
75 gm mushrooms - sliced finely (3/4 cup)
½ tbsp butter
1½ cups (150 gm) grated mozzarella or pizza cheese
3 tbsp cream
1 tbsp tomato puree, 1 tbsp cornflour
½ tsp salt, ¼ tsp ground pepper
2 tbsp chopped fresh parsley or coriander, ½ tsp dried oregano
1 small tomato - sliced into rings, a few olives - sliced, optional

1. Sift flour and baking powder. Combine butter with flour, rubbing well until it looks like bread crumbs. Add cheese. Add just enough water to bind and knead lightly to a firm dough. Chill the dough, well covered in a wet muslin cloth, for 15 minutes.
2. Roll out to a thin chappati, slightly bigger than the baking tin. If it gets difficult to roll up to the right size, roll out to a 5-6" inch round and place it in the flan tin. Press the mixture into a buttered 9 inch quiche or flan tin, pressing well to extend the dough and cover the base and a little of the sides too. Press carefully to get a well levelled base.
3. Prick with a fork all over to avoid the crust from puffing up during baking.
4. Bake the quiche crust in a hot oven (200°C/390°F), for about 15-20 minutes, until light golden brown. Allow to cool.
5. To prepare the filling, heat butter. Add mushrooms and cook until water evaporates and they turn dry. Add baby corns. Cook for a few seconds. Remove from fire.
6. In a cup, mix together — cream, tomato puree, cornflour, salt, pepper and parsley.
7. Spoon corn mixture into the cooled quiche crust, smooth out.
8. Sprinkle 1 cup grated cheese on it, keeping ½ cup for the top.
9. Spread the cream-tomato puree mixture on the cheese. Press the slices of tomato on top, sprinkle with the remaining cheese. Garnish with olives & remaining mushrooms, baby corns and parsley. Sprinkle some oregano.
10. Bake in a preheated oven set at 190°C/375°F for about 20 minutes or until the filling is set and the top is golden. Allow to cool before slicing.

Channa Masala

Serve with ready made kulchas.

CHANNA MASALA
1 cup channa kabuli (Bengal gram)
2 tbsp channe ki dal (split gram)
2 moti illaichi (big cardamoms)
1" stick dalchini (cinnamon)
2 tsp tea leaves tied in a muslin cloth or a tea bag
¼ tsp mitha soda (soda bicarb)
1" piece ginger
1 green chilli
1½ tsp anardana (pomegranate seeds) powder
2 onions - chopped finely
1 big tomato - chopped finely
½ tsp garam masala
1 tsp channa masala
1 tsp dhania powder
salt & red chilli powder to taste
4-5 tbsp oil

1. Soak channa & channe ki dal and enough water, overnight or for 6-8 hours in a pressure cooker. Next morning drain the water. Add about 3 cups fresh water and moti illaichi, dalchini, tea leaves and ¼ tsp soda-bicarb.
2. Pressure cook all the ingredients together to give one whistle. After the first whistle, keep on low flame for about 20 minutes. Keep aside.
3. Grind ginger, green chilli and anardana to a paste. Keep aside.
4. Heat oil. Add onions. Cook stirring till they turn dark brown. (Do not burn them). Add chopped tomatoes. Cook & mash occasionally till they turn brownish in colour.
5. Add dhania powder and red chilli powder. Cook for ½ minute.
6. Add ginger paste. Cook for ½ minute.
7. Remove tea bag from the boiled channas and add to the onion masala. Mix well. Add salt. Cook for 5-7 minutes. Add garam masala & channa masala. Mix well. Keep on low flame for 10-15 minutes.
8. At serving time, remove the whole spices from the channas and keep on fire till hot. Heat 2 tbsp oil on a tawa. Toss 1 tomato cut into 2 halves and 1 green chilli slit lengthways; for a few seconds in it. Add ½ tsp red chilli powder and pour over the hot channas in the serving dish.

Chicken Chaat

Serves 4

A cold summer preparation.

2 large chicken breasts - boiled & cubed
1 small firm tomato
½ capsicum
2 tender spring onions without greens
1 tsp chaat masala
¼ tsp kala namak (rock salt)
¼ tsp powdered sugar
salt and pepper to taste
juice of 1 lemon

1. Wash the chicken breast. Boil with ½ tsp salt and ½ cup water till tender or pressure cook with ½ cup water and ½ tsp salt to give 1 whistle. Debone the meat and cut into cubes.
2. Cut tomato. Remove pulp and cut into small cubes. Deseed capsicum and cut into small cubes.
3. Cut the white part of the spring onions in thin circles, discarding the green part.
4. Collect the chicken & vegetables in a bowl.
5. Sprinkle all the dry ingredients.
6. Squeeze lemon juice and toss.
7. Cover with a cling film and keep in the refrigerator to chill. If the chaat is not covered, the chicken tends to harden.
8. Serve on a bed of lettuce or cabbage.

Party Sandwich

Serves 10

COVERING
3/4 cups thick curd prepared from full cream milk
½ cup (100 gm) fresh cream, optional
salt, pepper to taste, 1 tsp powdered sugar

YELLOW CHEESE FILLING
50 gms paneer
2 tbsp finely grated cucumber or carrot
salt, pepper to taste
1 tbsp milk, few drops of yellow colour or a pinch haldi

RED TOMATO FILLING
2 tomatoes - pureed in a grinder, 2 tbsp tomato sauce
¼ tsp salt, ¼ tsp pepper

GREEN MINT CHUTNEY
(½ cup) ½ bunch poodina (mint) leaves
1 cup hara dhania (fresh coriander) leaves
1 green chilli, 1 onion - sliced
1 tsp sugar, salt and amchoor to taste

OTHER INGREDIENTS
12 slices of fresh bread (sides removed)
butter - enough to spread
fresh coriander leaves & a few black grapes for garnishing

1. Hang curd (prepared from full cream milk) for ½ hour in a thin muslin cloth. Beat cream with salt, sugar and pepper till thick and attains a soft dropping consistency. Keep in the fridge. Beat hung curd till smooth. Mix the whipped cream into the curd. If you do not wish to use cream, hang 1½ cups thick curd and whip hung curd with salt, sugar and pepper till smooth.
2. To prepare the yellow filling, grate paneer. Mix everything to make a paste of spreading consistency. Add some yellow colour. Keep filling aside.
3. Grind tomatoes to a puree in a mixer. Cook puree in a small pan till thick. Add tomato sauce, salt & pepper. Cook for 1 minute. Keep red filling aside.
4. Grind all ingredients of the mint chutney to a fine paste with the minimum amount of water to a thick paste.
5. In a longish serving plate, arrange 3 slices of bread joining each other.
6. Spread cheese filling on each slice. Butter 3 more slices and cover the cheese filling with the buttered side of the slices.

7. Spread green chutney generously. Cover with 3 buttered slices.
8. Spread red filling generously. Cover with 3 more buttered slices of bread.
9. Cover this loaf with beaten curd.
10. Draw a clean fork lengthwise on the curd, across the sandwich in the centre. Draw lines on the sides, along the height also with a fork.
11. Dip small coriander leaves in cold water for 10 minutes. Arrange 2 rows of open coriander leaves on both sides.
12. In the centre, place cherry or grape halves on the fork lines, if you like.
13. Cut a tomato slice into four pieces, arrange one on each corner.
14. Refrigerate for 1-2 hours or even more, before serving. To serve, cut into slices.

Unfried Moong Balls

Servings 20 balls

BALLS
1 cup dhuli moog dal (split green beans) - soaked for 2 hours
1 tsp salt, 4 tbsp oil

MASALA
2 tbsp oil
3 onions - chopped
2 tomatoes - chopped
½" ginger piece - grated, 2 green chillies - chopped
½ tsp salt, ¼ tsp garam masala (mixed spices), ¼ tsp red chilli powder

1. Soak dal for 2 hours. Drain the water and grind with minimum amount of water to a smooth paste.
2. Cook dal in 4 tbsp of oil in a kadhai for about 10 minutes on slow fire by sprinkling water occasionally. Cook till dal turns dry. Add salt.
4. Make marble sized balls with greased hands. Keep moog balls aside.
5. To prepare the masala, heat 2 tbsp oil in a kadhai.
6. Add onions. Cook till golden brown.
7. Add chopped tomatoes. Cook for 3-4 minutes.
8. Add ginger & green chillies.
9. Add salt, garam masala and red chilli powder. Add 2-3 tbsp of water. Cook for 1 minute. Keep aside till serving time.
10. At the time of serving, heat the masala and add the balls. Mix well till the balls are heated through. Serve sprinkled with chopped coriander.

Minty Mushroom Rolls

Serves 8-10

4 boiled potatoes - mashed or grated
2 slices of bread - sides removed and crumbled to get fresh crumbs
½ tsp garam masala, ½ tsp red chilli powder, salt to taste
oil for frying
bread crumbs to coat

FILLING
1 tbsp butter
150 gms mushrooms -chopped (1½ cups)
¼ cup finely chopped mint leaves
1 large onion - chopped
salt and pepper to taste

1   Boil potatoes. Mash well while still hot or grate them if they have turned cold.
2. Crumble the slices in a mixer or by hand to get fresh bread crumbs.
3. To the mashed potatoes, add bread, garam masala, red chilli powder and salt to taste. Keep aside.
4. To prepare the filling, heat butter in a pan. Add onions and cook till soft. Add mushrooms. Sauté for 3-4 minutes and let them turn dry.
5. Add mint, salt and pepper to taste. Mix well. Remove from heat.
6. Divide the potato mixture into 8 balls. Flatten each potato ball to a diameter of about 3 inches.
7. Place 1 tbsp of mushroom and mint filling on it. Press. Cover the filling by lifting the sides of the potato. Shape into a roll. Flatten the sides of the roll.
8. Roll over bread crumbs to coat.
9. Heat oil in a pan and fry till golden brown. Serve with tomato ketchup or hari chutney.

Savoury Mushroom Loaf

Serves 6

100 gms (1 cup) maida (plain flour)
2 big potatoes - boiled and grated (1½ cups potato paste)
1 tsp salt, ¼ tsp baking powder
2 semi heaped tbsp (¼ cup melted) butter or margarine, (do not use oil)

FILLING
3 tbsp oil
2 laung (cloves) - crushed
2 onions - chopped finely
½ packet (100 gms) mushrooms - sliced
1 tomato - chopped finely
1 green chilli - deseeded & chopped finely
salt and pepper to taste

1. Mix grated, boiled potatoes with maida in a bowl. Add salt and baking powder.
2. Melt ghee or margarine and pour over the maida. Mix well to form a firm dough. Add enough ghee to form a dough. Knead well. Chill in the fridge.
3. To prepare the filling, heat oil. Add onions. Cook till transparent.
4. Add sliced mushrooms and stir fry for 4-5 minutes on medium flame till brown and well cooked. Add laung & tomato. Cook for 2-3 minutes. Add green chillies. Add salt & pepper to taste. Cook till almost dry. Cool the filling.
5. To prepare the loaf, grease a flat baking tray generously.
6. Make 2 balls with the cold potato dough. Roll out one ball into a rectangular chappati, ¼" thick. Trim the sides neatly with a knife to get a neat rectangle.
7. Place on an aluminium foil lined and greased tray. Sprinkle a little maida. Spread the filling.
8. Mix trimmings with the second ball & roll out a bigger rectangle. Trim sides. Place it on the filling so as to cover the sides. Join the edges to form a loaf. Pinch edges. Brush with milk or egg mixed with a little water. Make slits ½" apart. Roll out the left over trimmings & cut petals. Make a flower with the petals on the loaf.
9. Bake in a heated oven at 170°C/325°F for 30-40 minutes, keeping the tray on the upper shelf because the loaf tends to turn brown faster at the bottom. Bake till golden brown. Serve hot.

Mango Chutney Submarine

Serves 4-5

1 long garlic bread - cut lengthwise to get 2 thin, long pieces
1 tbsp butter - softened
2 tbsp sweet mango chutney (fun food)

TOPPING
1 kheera - cut into round slices without peeling
2 firm tomatoes - cut into round slices
250 gm paneer - cut into ¼" thick, 1½" squares
few poodina (mint) leaves to garnish - dipped in chilled water
1 tbsp oil

SPRINKLE ON PANEER
¼ tsp haldi, ½ tsp chilli powder, ½ tsp salt, 1 tsp chaat masala powder

1. Spread butter on the cut surface of both the pieces of garlic bread.
2. Place the garlic breads in the oven at 200°C on a wire rack for 10-12 minutes till crisp and light brown on the cut surface. Keep aside.
3. Cut paneer into ¼" thick, big square pieces.
4. Sprinkle the paneer on both sides with some chilli powder, salt, haldi and chaat masala.
5. At serving time, heat 1 tbsp oil in a non stick pan. Saute paneer pieces on both sides in oil till slightly toasted to a nice yellowish-brown colour. Keep aside.
6. To assemble the submarine, apply 1 tbsp mango chutney on each garlic bread.
7. Sprinkle some chaat masala on the kheera and tomato pieces. Sprinkle some chat masala on the paneer also.
8. Place a piece of paneer at an angle, (pointed sided in the centre), then kheera, then tomato and keep repeating all three in the same sequence so as to cover the loaf. Keep paneer, kheera and tomato, slightly overlapping. Insert fresh mint leaves in between the paneer and vegetables, so that they show. Serve.

Note: Mango chutney is available in bottles in stores.

Kandhari Bhel

Serves 4

Spicy and delicious!

3 slices bread
chaat masala to taste, salt to taste
1 onion - chopped finely
2 green chillies - chopped finely, 1 tbsp chopped coriander
1 cup (50 gms) namkeen sev (Bikaneri Bhujiya)
1 cup red or kandhari annar ke dane (fresh red pomegranate seeds)
2 tbsp khatti mithi chutney (given below)
2 tbsp poodina (mint) ki chutney
oil for frying
lemon rings to serve

QUICK KHATTI MITHI CHUTNEY
1 tbsp amchoor (dried mango powder)
3 tbsp sugar or shakkar (gur)
½ tsp bhuna jeera (roasted cumin seeds) powder
¼ tsp red chilli powder, ¼ tsp salt, ¼ tsp garam masala
¼ cup water

1. Mix all ingredients of the khatti mithi chutney together in a small heavy bottomed pan. Cook on low flame, till all the ingredients dissolve properly and the chutney reaches the right consistency. Keep aside to cool.
2. Cut bread slices into (¼") tiny square pieces. Deep fry to a golden brown colour.
3. Mix onion, annar, green chillies and chopped coriander.
4. Sprinkle some chaat masala.
5. Add chutneys to taste. Mix well.
6. Add fried bread cubes and the sev in the end just before serving otherwise the bhel turns soggy.
7. Arrange one or two cabbage leaves in a bowl. Fill the prepared bhelpuri and sprinkle some more sev and annar on top.
8. Serve immediately, garnished with lemon rings otherwise it tends to get soggy.

Amritsari Machhi

Serves 4-6   *Picture on facing page*

500 gm River Sole or Singhara fish - boneless, cut in 2" pieces

1ST MARINADE
2-3 tbsp malt vinegar
or
2 tbsp lemon juice
½ tsp red chilli powder
salt to taste

2ND MARINADE
2 tbsp ginger-garlic paste
½ tsp ajwain (carom seeds)
¼ tsp red chilli powder
3 tbsp besan (gram flour)
2 tbsp maida or cornflour
salt to taste
a few drops orange red colour
chat masala to sprinkle
oil for frying

1. Wash the fish and pat dry on a kitchen towel.
2. Marinate the fish in the 1st marinade for ½ hour.
3. Remove the fish from 1st marinade and pat dry again. If there is excess moisture, the fish will not fry crisp.
4. In a bowl, mix ginger-garlic paste, ajwain, chilli powder, salt and colour. Mix well and add to the fish pieces. Keep aside for marination till frying time.
5. At the time of frying, sprinkle dry besan and cornflour on the marinated fish. Mix well.
6. Heat oil in a kadhai. Fry 4-5 pieces of fish at a time on medium heat till the pieces are crisp. Drain on absorbent paper.
7. Arrange fish pieces on a serving platter. Garnish with lemon rings, onion rings and mint leaves. Serve hot with mint chutney.

Til Mil Paneer

Serves 3-4 *Picture on back cover*

200 gms paneer

BATTER
4 tbsp maida (plain flour)
2-3 flakes garlic - crushed
1/3 cup water (approx.)
½ tsp red chilli powder
½ tsp chaat masala
½ tsp salt to taste

COATING
1/3 cup bread crumbs
4 tbsp til (sesame seeds)
1 tbsp suji (semolina)
a pinch of dry orange red colour
oil for frying

1. Cut the paneer into slices of ¼" thickness. Cut the slices diagonally to get triangles. Sprinkle salt or chaat masala on both sides. Keep aside.
2. Heat oil on medium heat in a kadhai.
3. Mix all the ingredients of the batter in a shallow flat bowl.
4. Mix all the coating ingredients in large flat plate, to spread out the mixture. (See note.)
5. Dip the paneer pieces in the batter. Remove from batter and toss in the coating mixture to coat all sides.
6. Fry the paneer pieces, one at a time, till crisp. Drain on a paper napkins to absorb excess oil. Serve hot.

Note: The coating mixture should be spread out in a plate and not in a bowl, so that when the paneer pieces are being coated, the whole mixture does not turn soggy.

Spinach & Mushroom Pie

Servings 8

SHORT CRUST PASTRY (DOUGH)
200 gms maida (plain flour)
100 gms butter - chilled
½ tsp salt, a big pinch of baking powder
4-5 tbsp ice cold water

FILLING
250 gms (2 cups) chopped palak (spinach)
100 gms (10-12) mushrooms - chopped
2 onions - chopped finely, 1 tomato - chopped finely, 2 green chillies - chopped finely
2 tbsp oil
salt, pepper to taste, ½ tsp red chilli powder
1 tbsp cream or malai

1. Sift flour & salt. Add chilled butter. With a fork, break butter gently and mix with the maida. Mix gently with a fork and do not use your hands, because the heat of the hand will make the pie hard on baking. Then rub quickly & lightly with the finger tips till the flour resembles bread crumbs. See that the butter does not melt.
2. Sprinkle water evenly over the flour.
3. Knead lightly to a firm dough of rolling consistency. Chill the dough in a polythene bag or wrapped up in a wet cloth for 15 minutes.
4. Roll out the dough in one direction only to 1/8" thick, without stretching. The size should be 3" bigger than the baking dish.
5. Grease a 7-8" borosil glass dish or a flat tin with a loose bottom. Line it with the rolled out pastry, such that it covers the bottom and the sides. Cut the sides in level with the dish. Pinch the sides to give a fluted edging.
6. Prick the sides and the bottom with a fork.
7. Bake blind (empty) in a hot oven at 210°C for 15-20 minutes till light brown.
8. Remove the pie shell from the dish after 10 minutes. If it is difficult to remove the pie shell, leave it in the dish. Keep aside.
9. To prepare the filling, heat oil. Add onions & cook till transparent. Add tomatoes & green chilli. Cook for 3-4 minutes.
10. Add washed spinach & mushrooms. Cover and cook for 5-7 minutes till done.
11. Add red chilli, salt, pepper and cream. Cook till dry. Remove from fire. Cool.
12. At serving time, fill the filling in the baked pie shell. Reheat in the oven. To serve, cut into slices.

Vegetable Rava Idli

Makes 5 idlis

1 tbsp oil
a pinch hing (asfoetida)
½ tsp rai (mustard seeds)
1-2 green chillies - chopped finely
1 cup suji (rawa)
a few curry leaves
½ of a small carrot - chopped very finely (¼ cup)
4 french beans - threaded and chopped very finely
3/4 tsp eno fruit salt
1 cup curd
½ cup water
3/4 tsp salt

1. Heat 1 tbsp oil in a heavy bottomed kadhai.
2. Add hing, rai and green chillies. Wait for 1 minute.
3. Add vegetables (carrots and beans) and saute for 2 minutes.
4. Add suji (rawa). Mix well. Stir fry for 2 minutes on low heat.
5. Add curry leaves and salt. Mix well. Remove from fire. Allow to cool for 2-3 minutes.
6. Transfer to a bowl. Add curd, water & eno fruit salt. Beat well.
7. Grease an idli stand. Pour 2-3 tbsp mixture into each mould.
8. To steam, put 1" water in a big pressure cooker or a big pan with a well fitting lid and keep it on fire.
9. Place the idli mould inside the cooker & put the lid after removing the whistle. Keep the gas on full flame.
10. After the water boils and the steam starts coming out, reduce flame. Keep for 15 minutes on medium flame.
11. Switch off the fire. Wait for 5 minutes and then remove the idlis from the mould with a clean knife.
12. Serve hot with coconut chutney as given on page 116.

Mutton Balls

Serves 4-6

½ kg fine keema (lamb mince)
2 tbsp garlic-ginger-green chilli paste
1 tsp garam masala
1 tsp dhania powder (ground coriander)
1 tsp red chilli powder, salt to taste
2 tbsp heaped besan (gram flour)
4 tbsp oil for shallow frying

DRY MASALA COATING
½ tsp chat masala
1 tbsp dhania powder
1 tsp red chilli powder
1 tsp garam masala

1. Put the mince in a strainer. Pour water to wash and gently press to drain out all the water (if water is not drained out properly, the balls will not bind well and tend to break while pressure cooking).
2. Put the mince in a bowl. Add all the other ingredients except oil. Mix and knead well or put in a mixer blender and blend well.
3. Take a pressure cooker or a pan, oil its bottom well.
4. Take a heaped tbsp of mince in the palm of your hand and bind the mince tightly into balls, squeezing out any excess liquid. Make balls a little bag, as mince tends to shrink after cooking.
5. Arrange them at the bottom of the pressure cooker. Place the balls gently, over lapping one another, if short of space. Do not add water in the cooker, as the mince will leave water.
6. Pressure cook to give 2 whistles and simmer on low flame for 2 minutes. Remove from fire. Let the pressure drop by itself.
7. Gently remove the steamed meat balls. Keep aside.
8. At serving time, add 4 tbsp oil in a non stick pan and shallow fry the steamed balls in a pan on medium heat.
9. When they turn brown, add chaat masala, coriander powder, red chilli powder and garam masala. Cook till dry masala coats the balls.
10. Remove to a plate and garnish with green coriander and lemon wedges. Serve with coriander or mint chutney.

Paneer & Corn Dumplings

Serves 8

FILLING
½ cup corn kernels (tinned) - drain liquid
200 gm paneer - roughly mashed (1½ cups)
1 onion - chopped very finely
2-3 green chillies - deseeded and chopped finely
¼ cup chopped coriander
1 tsp salt, or to taste
½ tsp each of red chilli powder, pepper powder and amchoor, or to taste

OTHER INGREDIENTS
10 -12 slices of bread
oil for frying

1. Mash paneer roughly. Add all other ingredients of the filling. Keep aside.
2. Dip a bread slice in a bowl of water for a second. Keep it flat on the palm and press between the palms to squeeze out all the water.
3. Place a heaped tbsp of filling and cover with the bread to form a roll.
4. Heat oil. Fry one roll at a time till golden brown and crisp. Drain from oil and cut vertically into two pieces to get roundish pieces. Serve hot.

Keema Bread Rolls

Serves 4

8 slices bread
250 gm cooked keema
1 capsicum - deseeded and chopped
1 onion - chopped finely, 1 green chilli - chopped finely
2 tbsp finely chopped green coriander
oil for frying

1. Mix capsicum, onion, green chilli, coriander with the cooked keema.
2. Trim the sides of the slices. Dip a slice in water and place between the palms of the hands and gently squeeze excess water.
3. Place (2 spoon full) stuffing in the center and shape into oblong rolls. Repeat with all the other slices. Keep aside.
4. Heat oil in a kadhai. Deep fry the rolls to golden brown in hot oil. Drain on a paper napkin. Serve hot on bed of lettuce with ketchup.

Drums of Heaven

Serves 4-6   *Picture on page 99*

12 chicken wings - made into lollipops
2 tbsp soya sauce
1 tbsp ginger-garlic paste
½ tsp red chilli paste or powder
¼ tsp pepper, salt to taste
pinch of ajinomoto (optional)
oil for deep frying
lemon twists and coriander to garnish

BATTER (MIX TOGETHER)
1 egg
2 tbsp maida
1 tbsp cornflour
pinch of each - salt, pepper, ajimomoto and dry orange red colour

1. Marinate the chicken wings with soya sauce, ginger-garlic paste, chilli paste, salt, pepper and ajinomoto for 3-4 hours. Keep in the refrigerator.
2. Mix all ingredients of the batter.
3. Heat oil in a kadhai. Dip the chicken wings in the batter and fry on medium hot oil till golden and crisp.
4. Garnish the serving platter with lemon twists and coriander leaves. Serve hot wings with chilli sauce.

Spinach Mushroom Pancakes

Serves 6-7

2 cups maida (plain flour)
1 egg
1½ cups milk
250 gm spinach
½ tsp soda bicarb, ½ tsp baking powder
3/4 tsp salt

TOPPING
200 gm mushrooms - sliced thickly
1 tomato - sliced without pulp
2 spring onions with greens - chopped
1 tbsp oil
salt and pepper to taste

1. Cut the stems of the spinach and blanch leaves for 2 minutes in boiling water. Strain and squeeze excess water. Chop leaves finely.
2. Mix maida, egg, milk, spinach, soda, baking powder, salt and pepper well. Keep aside for ½ hour.
3. To prepare the topping, heat oil in a non stick pan. Add spring onions and stir for ½ minute. Add mushrooms, stir for 1 minute, add tomato, salt and pepper. Mix and remove from fire. (The salt is added at the end. If salt is added earlier, the mushrooms leave water). Keep aside.
4. To prepare pancakes, heat a non-stick tawa. Coat tawa with ½ tsp oil.
5. Keeping the flame on medium, drop 1 heaped tbsp of batter. Gently spread to make a small thickish pancake (pancake should not be thin).
6. When the bottom get cooked, turn the pancake to cook the other side. Remove on a serving dish.
7. Make 2-3 pancakes at a time on the tawa.
8. Top the pancakes with 1 tbsp of hot mushroom topping. Serve hot.

Note : When you want to make half the quantity, say with 1 cup maida, add 1 whole egg, but reduce the quantity of milk, adding just enough to get a thick pouring consistency.

Pao Bhaji

Servings 7-8

This delicious bhaji served with buns, is really relishing as well filling.

250 gms (3 big) potatoes - boiled
4 tomatoes - chopped
3 onions - chopped finely
2 tbsp Pao-Bhaji Masala
50 gms butter, 4-5 tbsp oil
1½ tsp salt, or to taste
1 tbsp chopped coriander

PRESSURE COOK TOGETHER
2 cups chopped cabbage
½ cup shelled peas, ½ cup chopped cauliflower
½ cup chopped brinjals, any variety, 1 cup chopped carrots

GRIND TO A PASTE
1" piece ginger, 4-6 flakes garlic - optional, 2-4 green chillies

TO SERVE
pao (buns) - cut into halves, butter - enough to spread
1 onion - sliced finely
yogurt minty dip - page 113

1. Chop all vegetables. Mash boiled potatoes roughly.
2. Pressure cook all vegetables together with ½ cup water to give one whistle. Remove from fire.
3. Grind ginger, garlic and green chillies to a paste.
4. Heat oil. Add onions and cook till transparent.
5. Add ginger paste and cook for 2-3 minutes on low flame.
6. Add pao-bhaji masala and salt.
7. Add tomatoes and cook covered for 6-8 minutes. Mash them well.
8. Add pressure cooked vegetables and potatoes. Cook for a 6-8 minutes, mashing them continuously. Keep aside till serving time.
9. At serving time heat the bhaji. Add butter and chopped coriander.
10. Mix the finely sliced onions in yogurt minty dip and keep aside.
11. To serve, cut buns into half. Spread some butter on them on the cut side and press lightly on a hot tawa till heated well.
12. Serve hot pao-bhaji sprinkled with fresh coriander and a dollop of butter, along with hot buns and some onions in chutney.

Kashmiri Lamb Chops

Serves 4-6   *Picture on facing page*

10-12 lamb chops (500 gm) - each lamb chop is about 50 gm
2 cups milk
50 gm khoya
1 tej patta (bay leaf)

BOUQUET GARNI (TIE TOGETHER IN A MUSLIN CLOTH)
1" stick dalchini (cinnamon stick)
1 tsp saunf (fennel)
2-3 chhoti illachi (green cardamom)
½ tsp saboot kali mirch (peppercorns)

BATTER
2/3 cup curd
2 tbsp maida (flour)
½ tsp garam masala
3-4 flakes garlic or 1" piece ginger - crushed to a paste
½ tsp salt, a pinch of haldi
oil for frying

1. Wash the chops and gently beat the meat on the chops with a mallet to break the fibres.
2. Place the chops with 2 cups of milk, bay leaf and bouquet garni in a pressure cooker. Pressure cook to give 2 whistles and keep on low heat for 1 minute. Remove from fire. Cool and open the lid.
3. Add the khoya and salt, simmer till the chops are cooked and the milk is absorbed by the chops.
4. Discard the bouquet garni and the bay leaf.
5. Make a batter by blending curd, flour, chilli, salt, garam masala and garlic or ginger in a bowl. Add a little haldi for colour. The batter should be of a coating consistency.
6. Heat oil in a kadhai. Lower the heat.
7. Dip each chop in batter. Fry on low or medium heat till the chops are golden brown. Drain on absorbent paper.
8. Serve hot garnished with a mint sprig and lemon wedges.

Snacks From
AROUND THE WORLD

Chinese Potato Rolls

Serves 8

ROLLS
4 medium potatoes - boiled and mashed well
2 tsp khus-khus (poppy seeds)
3 tbsp cornflour
1 green chilli - deseed and chopped
2 tbsp chopped coriander
¼ tsp amchoor, 3/4 tsp salt, ½ tsp pepper

CHINESE SAUCE
1 tbsp oil
6-8 flakes garlic - crushed
1 green chilli - deseeded and chopped
2 tbsp tomato sauce
1½ tbsp soya sauce
1 tsp red chilli sauce
¼ tsp pepper, ¼ tsp salt
2 tbsp chopped coriander
1 tsp cornflour dissolved in 1/3 cup water

1. Mash and mix potatoes with all the ingredients given under rolls.
2. With wet hands, shape into small rolls, of about 1" size. Make the sides flat.
3. Deep fry in medium hot oil to golden brown. Keep aside.
4. For the sauce, heat 1 tbsp oil in a pan. Reduce flame. Add garlic and green chillies.
5. When garlic changes colour remove from fire.
6. Add tomato sauce, chilli sauce and soya sauce. Return to fire and add salt, pepper. Cook the sauces for ½ minute.
7. Add cornflour dissolved in water. Add chopped coriander.
8. Simmer for a minute till thick.
9. Add the fried rolls and stir till the sauce coats the rolls, for about 1 minute. Serve hot.

Note: Advance work can be done upto step 7, but thicken the sauce and add the rolls to the sauce at the time of serving. If the rolls are in the sauce for too long, they turn limp.

Thai Chicken Satay

(Chicken on Skewers)

Serves 6   *Picture on page 2*

400 gm chicken - bite sized boneless pieces
6 bamboo skewers - soaked in water to prevent burning

MARINADE
1 tsp salt, ½-1 tsp red chilli powder
2 tsp brown sugar
1 tbsp lemon juice
2 tsp soya sauce
8-10 flakes garlic - crushed to a paste
2 tsp oil
1½ tsp jeera powder (ground cumin), 1½ tsp dhania powder (ground coriander)
3-4 tbsp coconut milk (ready made - Dabur)

PEANUT SAUCE
¼ cup (50 gm) roasted salted peanuts, ½ tsp salt
1 tsp oil, 4-6 flakes garlic - crushed
½ tsp red chilli powder
½-1 tsp sugar, 1½ tsp lemon juice, 1 tsp soya sauce
1 cup coconut milk

1. Mix all the marinade ingredients thoroughly, add chicken pieces to it and mix very well. Leave aside for 1-2 hours in the refrigerator.
2. Thread marinated chicken pieces onto oiled wooden skewers. Leave behind the marinade.
3. Cook in a preheated grill at 230°C for 10-11 minutes, turning them once in between and basting with the remaining marinade. Alternately, heat a non-stick flat tawa, grease it slightly with a few drops of oil and place skewered chicken, a few at a time. Cook on high heat, turning them frequently. Cook till soft.
4. To make the peanut sauce, grind the peanuts with the salt to a rough powder.
5. Heat oil in a heavy bottomed small pan or kadhai. Add garlic. Saute till it starts to change colour. Reduce heat. Add red chilli powder. Add only ½ cup coconut milk. Boil, stirring. Cook on low heat for 3 minutes, stirring constantly. Stir in the crushed peanuts, sugar, lemon juice, soya sauce and the remaining ½ cup coconut milk. Boil. Simmer gently for 5 minutes, stirring occasionally to prevent it sticking to the pan. Transfer to a bowl.
6. Serve satay accompanied with the peanut sauce.

Chicken Spring Rolls

Serves 4

1 egg
4 tbsp maida (plain flour)
4 tbsp cornflour
a pinch of salt
½ cup water, approx.

FILLING
1 chicken breast - boiled and shredded
½ cup cabbage - finely shredded
¼ cup grated carrot
½ capsicum - shredded
1 spring onion - finely shredded upto the greens
4-5 flakes garlic - crushed and chopped
1 tsp soya sauce
¼ tsp pepper, salt to taste
a pinch of ajinomoto (optional)
oil for frying

1. Mix egg, cornflour, maida and salt in a bowl. Pour about ½ cup of water to make a batter of pouring consistency. Beat well to get a smooth batter.
2. Heat a non stick pan. Pour a serving spoon full of batter and roll the pan to get a thin pancake. Cook on medium heat. Remove the pancake when cooked. Do not turn. Cook only on one side. Make 3-4 more pancakes with the remaining batter. Keep pancakes aside.
3. To prepare the filling, place the chicken breast with ¼ cup water and a little salt in a pressure cooker and give 1 whistle. Remove from heat. Cool and shred chicken into very small pieces.
4. Heat 2 tbsp oil in a pan. Add garlic. Stir, add the spring onion, cabbage, carrot, capsicum and chicken. Stir, add salt, pepper, soya sauce and ajinomoto. Remove from heat and cool.
5. Keeping the uncooked side down, place little filling little away from one end on the cooked side. Fold the sides in, roll up neatly enclosing the filling. Seal the edge with leftover batter or egg white. Keep aside.
6. Heat oil (3/4 cup) in a frying pan and deep fry the roll to golden brown and crisp. Cut into 3-4 pieces. Serve hot with hot garlic dip or ketchup.

Italian Minty Prawns

Serves 5-6

A delicious mint flavoured snack.

300 gms big prawns (shell & devein them keeping their tails intact)

MARINADE
3 tbsp lemon juice
4-5 tbsp finely chopped or minced mint leaves
1½ tsp salt
1½ tsp pepper or red chilli powder

BATTER
¾ cup flour (maida)
¾ cup luke warm water
¾ tsp salt
¾ tsp pepper or red chilli powder
¼ tsp dry yeast

1. Mix all ingredients given under marinade. Add prawns. Mix well. Leave for ½-1 hour.
2. For the batter, mix together flour, salt, red chilli powder and yeast. Add luke warm water (the water should hot be too hot or cold or the yeast will not rise). Mix well so that no lumps remain. Keep aside for ½ hour. The batter will rise and become soft and fluffy.
3. Heat oil. Dip each prawn into the batter and deep fry a few at a time till golden brown. Serve hot with tomato or chilli sauce.

VARIATION

- 2" piece of boneless chicken, chicken with bones cut into small pieces, egg plant cut into round slices, cauliflower florets, baby corns can be used instead of prawns.

- Instead of mint. chopped parsely/dhania can be used.

Honey Chilli Baby Corns

Serves 4

100 gm baby corns (12-15 big ones)

BATTER
3 tbsp cornflour, 2 tbsp maida (plain flour)
1 egg or 3-4 tbsp water
1 tsp vinegar, 1 tsp soya sauce
1/3 tsp salt, 1/3 tsp pepper
¼ tsp ajinomoto, ¼ tsp baking powder
4-5 flakes garlic - crushed
1 tbsp hot oil
oil for frying

OTHER INGREDIENTS
4-5 green chillies - cut lengthwise, deseeded and then cut into thin long pieces
4-5 flakes crushed garlic - optional
1 tbsp chopped coriander
2 tsp soya sauce, 1 tbsp tomato sauce, 1 tbsp vinegar
1½ tsp honey
¼ tsp each of salt and pepper

1. Mix all ingredients of the batter to make a batter of a thick coating consistency. Add 1-2 tbsp water as required. Keep aside.
2. Slit baby corns into 2 halves lengthwise if big and thick or keep them whole if small. Boil 2 cups water with 1 tsp salt and a pinch of haldi for colour. Add baby corns. Boil for 1 minute. Drain and refresh in cold water. Pat dry on a kitchen towel.
3. Heat oil in a kadhai for frying.
4. Dip each babycorn in the batter and deep fry 5-6 together to a golden brown colour. Keep aside till serving time.
5. At the time of serving, heat 2 tbsp oil. Fry the green chillies and garlic for a few seconds. Remove from fire.
6. Add soya sauce, tomato sauce, vinegar and honey. Add salt and pepper. Stir.
7. Add the fried baby corns and coriander. Mix well. Serve hot.

Spaghetti & Corn Balls

Serves 4   *Picture on page 119*

1 cup boiled spaghetti
½ cup cooked corn kernels (tinned or freshly boiled)
2-3 tbsp grated mozzarella cheese
½ tsp saboot kali mirch (peppercorns) - crushed
4-6 flakes garlic - crushed
1 onion - finely chopped
2 tbsp chopped parsley or coriander
2 fresh red or green chillies - deseeded and chopped
2 tbsp butter
½ tsp salt
2½ tbsp maida (plain flour)
3/4 cup milk

COATING BATTER
¼ cup maida
1/3 cup water
a pinch of salt and pepper

1. Heat butter. Add flour. Stir on low heat for a minute.
2. Add garlic and onion. Cook on low heat for 2 minutes till onions turn soft. Add red or green chillies. Add chopped coriander or parsley.
3. Reduce heat and add milk, stirring continuously. Mix well and cook on medium flame, stirring continuously till thick.
4. Add corn. Mix well. Add salt and pepper to taste.
5. Add boiled spaghetti and cook further till very thick and lumpy.
6. Add cheese. Remove from fire and cool.
7. Make balls with greased hands, only after the mixture turns cold.
8. Heat oil till medium hot.
9. Prepare a thick coating batter with maida and water mixed together. Add a little salt and pepper.
10. Dip each ball in the coating batter and deep fry 3-4 pieces at a time, to a golden brown colour. Serve hot with tomato ketchup.

Thai Golden Pouches

Gives 15 pouches   *Picture on cover*

DOUGH
1 cup maida, ½ cup suji
a pinch of soda-bicarb, ½ tsp salt
1 tbsp oil & oil for frying

MEAT FILLING
1 tbsp butter/oil
225 gms mince (mutton or chicken or pork)
1 tbsp chopped fresh coriander, ½ to 1 tbsp chopped garlic
2 tbsp chopped spring onion/onion
½ tsp salt or adjust to taste, 1 tsp red chilli powder, 1 tsp sugar/gur
some freshly ground pepper (optional), 1 tbsp fish sauce

1. Heat oil in a pressure cooker. Add garlic. Fry for 1-2 minutes.
2. Add mince, salt, red chilli paste & 3-4 tbsp water.
3. Give 3-4 whistles. Cool and open the cooker. Add all the other ingredients, seasonings and dry completely on fire. Adjust seasonings to taste. Keep aside.
4. Mix all ingredients of the dough to make a dough with water (like chapati dough).
5. Make small balls around 15 and roll one at a time into a small rounds.
6. Put a teaspoon of filling in the centre & pick up the sides and press at the neck to form a money pouch. Tie the neck with a thin blade of lemon grass.
7. Deep fry till golden brown. Serve hot with peanut sauce given on page 72.

Vegetarian Pouches

VEGETARIAN FILLING
2 boiled potatoes - mashed roughly, 2 tbsp grated carrots
2 tbsp roasted peanuts - pounded
1 tsp soya sauce, ½ tsp sugar, ½ tsp salt

CRUSH TOGETHER
1 tsp chopped garlic, ½ tsp peppercorns, 1 tsp chopped coriander, 1 green chilli

1. Heat 1 tbsp oil. Reduce heat and add the crushed garlic etc. Stir for a few seconds.
2. Add carrots and mix.
3. Add potatoes, soya sauce, salt and sugar. Cook for 2-3 minutes. Add peanuts. Mix well. Remove from fire and proceed from step 4 given above.

Mexican Burrito

Serves 6-8   *Picture on facing page*

DOUGH
1 cup maida (plain flour), 1 cup atta (wheat flour)
¼ tsp salt, 3 tsp oil

RAJMAH FILLING
3/4 cup red rajmah (kidney beans) - soaked overnight or for 5-6 hours
1 dry red chilli, 1 tbsp oil, 3/4 tsp salt, 1 tbsp butter
1 onion - finely chopped, 2 flakes garlic - finely chopped, optional

HOT SAUCE
1 tbsp oil, 5 red tomatoes - blanched & chopped finely
½ tsp ajwain (carom seeds), 2 onions - finely chopped, 3-4 flakes garlic - finely chopped
3/4 tsp salt & pepper, 3 dry red chillies - soaked in ¼ cup water
2 tbsp tomato sauce

SOUR CREAM
3/4 cup thick curd - tied for ½ hour in a cloth and whipped till smooth
½ cup cream - whipped till thick
½ tsp salt, few drops tabasco sauce, a few spring onions for garnish

1. Boil soaked rajmah along with red chillies.
2. Sieve maida & atta. Add salt and oil. Knead to a soft dough with warm water.
3. For the sauce, soak dry red chillies in ¼ cup water for 15 minutes.
4. Mash chillies. Dip tomatoes in hot water for 10 min. Remove skin. Chop finely.
5. To prepare the sauce, heat oil. Add ajwain. Add garlic & onions. Fry till they turn transparent. Add tomatoes and mashed red chillies along with water. Cook till tomatoes turn pulpy. Mash well. Add salt and 2 tbsp tomato sauce. Cook for 7-10 minutes. Keep the hot sauce aside.
6. To prepare the filling, heat oil. Cook onions and garlic till pink. Add boiled rajmah, 2 tbsp of the prepared hot sauce, butter and salt. Cook for 5 minutes. Remove from fire and mash coarsely.
7. Beat hung curd well till smooth. Add salt, tobasco sauce and cream. Mix.
8. Make 8 small balls of the prepared dough. Roll out very thin chappatis.
9. Cook the chappatis on a tawa, keeping the cooked chappatis soft in a casserole.
10. At the time of serving, heat the rajmah filling, spread little filling on the chappati. Pour a little hot sauce & then sour cream over the rajmah.
11. Fold sides and roll up. Fry in very little oil (1 tbsp oil) in a non-stick pan or a tawa till crisp. Serve hot topped with extra hot sauce & sour cream. Garnish with spring onions.

Fragrant Thai Meat balls

Gives 24-25 balls

These tasty meat balls can be made from minced mutton or pork or chicken.

500 gms mince
1 tbsp chopped garlic
4-5 spring onions - finely chopped or 2 medium onions - chopped
1 tbsp chopped fresh coriander
4-5 tbsp red curry paste, recipe given below (ready made is also available)
1 tbsp lemon juice
1 tbsp fish sauce (optional)
1 tsp salt
½ tsp pepper
1 egg
rice flour for dusting
oil for deep frying
sprigs of coriander for garnishing

1. Wash mince. Squeeze out all the water by putting in a strainer and pressing well.
2. Mix all ingredients except rice flour & oil. Churn or grind in the mixer or mix well with hands.
3. Make balls, roll in the rice flour and deep fry.
4. Serve hot, garnished with sprigs of coriander.

Note: Instead of rice flour, powdered bread crumbs or suji can be used for rolling meat balls.

RED CURRY PASTE
Gives 1¾ cup

12-13 dried, red Kashmiri chillies - soaked in water for 15-20 minutes
3 tbsp chopped onion, 4 tbsp chopped garlic, 2 tbsp chopped ginger
2-3 lemon leaves, 4 sticks lemon grass - cut into pieces
1 tbsp coriander leaves , 20 peppercorns (saboot kali mirch)
1 tbsp coriander seeds (saboot dhania), 1 tbsp cumin seeds (jeera)
1 tsp shrimp paste (optional)

1. On a tawa, dry roast cumin and coriander seeds for about 5 minutes till they become aromatic and get roasted but not too brown. Grind finely.
2. Put all the other ingredients in a grinder and churn well to get a fine paste.
3. Mix in ground coriander and cumin and churn to mix. Store in a steel box or a glass jar in the fridge. The paste can be kept for a few days, about 8-10 days.

Vegetable Spring Rolls

Serves 4

PANCAKES

WITH EGG
½ cup flour
1 cup water
¼ tsp salt
1 egg
oil for shallow frying

WITHOUT EGG
½ cup flour
1 cup milk
¼ tsp salt
a pinch of soda-bi carb
oil for shallow frying

FILLING
1 onion - chopped finely
½ carrot-shredded, 8 french beans-parboiled
½ cup shredded cabbage, ½ cup shredded capsicum
½ cup bean sprouts
a pinch of ajinomoto
½ tsp white pepper, ½ tsp sugar, salt to taste
1 tsp soya sauce
2 tbsp oil

1. Sift flour and salt. Add water or milk gradually, beating well to make a smooth thin batter for pan cakes. Add egg or soda bicarb. Mix well.
2. Heat a non-stick pan (not too hot). Pour half the batter on it. Tilt the pan to spread the batter evenly.
3. Remove when the underside is cooked. Do not cook the other side.
4. Cool the two pancakes on dry cloth.
5. To prepare the filling, string french beans and drop into boiling water with ½ tsp salt for one minute. Strain. Cool. Shred diagonally. Shred all the other vegetables.
6. Heat oil. Add onions and sprouts & stir fry for 1 minute.
7. Add ajinomoto, salt pepper & sugar.
8. Add all other vegetables. Stir fry for 1 minute.
9. Add soya sauce and mix well.
10. Place half of the filling on the cooked side of the pancake, at one end which is nearest to you.
11. Fold the left side and then the right side. Holding the sides, roll upwards.
12. Seal the edges with cornflour paste, made by dissolving 1 tsp of cornflour in 1 tsp of water.
13. Heat some oil in a pan. Shallow fry both sides of the roll till golden brown.
14. Drain on absorbent paper. Cut diagonally into 1" pieces. Serve hot.

Chicken Burrito

Serves 4-6

½ cup cornflour, 1½ cups maida (plain flour)
1 large potato - boiled and grated
2 tbsp oil
½ tsp salt

FILLING
500 gm boneless chicken - cut into thin long strips
2 tbsp worcestershire sauce
1 tbsp soya sauce, 1 tbsp vinegar
1 tsp red chilli flakes or red chilli paste
3 tbsp oil
6-8 garlic flakes - chopped
2-3 spring onions - chopped diagonally
1 capsicum - deseeded and sliced

SOUR CREAM
½ cup cream (100 gm), 1 tsp lemon juice
1½ cups thick curd - hung for ½ hour in a muslin cloth
salt to taste

1. Mix maida, cornflour, grated boiled potato, oil and salt. Add just enough water and knead to a soft dough. Cover and keep aside.
2. For the filling, marinate the chicken with worcestershire sauce, soya sauce, vinegar and chilli paste or flakes and salt for ½ hour.
3. Heat oil in a non-stick pan. Add garlic, stir. Add the chicken, cook on high heat for 1 minute. Reduce heat. Cover and cook till chicken is tender. Add the capsicum and spring onion. Stir. Remove from heat.
4. For the sour cream, beat cream till stiff. Beat hung curd till smooth. Add to the cream. Stir in salt and lemon juice. Keep in the refrigerator.
5. Roll out thin 6"- 7" diameter chappati. Cook chappatis on a hot tawa on both sides on medium heat. Keep them warm in a casserole.
6. At the time of serving, heat 1 tbsp oil on a tawa. Fry the cooked chappati. Remove from heat. Spread hot chicken filling at one end. Spoon 1 tbsp of sour cream over the filling. Roll the chappati.
7. Serve hot with left over sour cream and salsa, given on page 115.

Hot & Sour Garlic Fish

Serves 8-10

500 gm boneless fish (Singhara or Sole) - cut into 1" cubes
1 tsp lemon juice or vinegar
salt to taste
1 spring onion - chopped, for garnish
oil for frying

BATTER (MIX TOGETHER)
2 eggs
4-5 tbsp maida, 2 tbsp oil or melted butter
salt & pepper to taste

SAUCE
2-3 tbsp oil
2 tbsp garlic - crushed & chopped
2 dried chillies - broken into small pieces
½ cup tomato puree
¼ cup tomato sauce
1 tsp soya sauce
a pinch of ajinomoto
salt to taste

1. Cut fish into small pieces of about 1" size cubes. Wash and pat dry fish. Marinate the fish in lemon juice and salt for ½ hour.
2. Mix all the ingredients of the batter to get a smooth batter of coating consistency.
3. Heat oil in a kadhai. Dip the fish pieces in batter and fry on medium heat. Remove on an absorbent paper.
4. In a clean non stick pan, heat 2-3 tbsp oil. Add garlic. Saute till it slightly changes colour.
5. Add the broken red chillies. Stir, add tomato puree, tomato sauce. soya sauce, salt and sugar.
5. Add the fish pieces and 2-3 tbsp water or fish stock. Stir till the sauce coats the fish pieces.
6. Remove on a platter. Garnish with chopped spring onions. Insert a toothpick in each piece and serve hot.

Note: You can add 1 tsp chilli paste in the sauce, if you want it to be more hot.

Batter Fried Chilli Chicken

Serves 6-8

Cut the chicken into small pieces as they become larger in size when coated with a flour-egg batter and deep fried.

1 chicken (700-800 gms) - cut into small pieces (14-16 pieces)
or
400-500 gms boneless chicken - cut into 1½" pieces
oil for frying

EGG BATTER
2 eggs
2 tbsp cornflour
2 tbsp maida
½ tsp pepper powder
½ tsp ajinomoto (optional)
½ tsp salt
pinch of baking powder

SAUCE
3 tbsp crushed & chopped garlic
4-5 green chillies - finely chopped
3 tbsp soya sauce
1 tbsp red chilli paste
2 tbsp tomato ketchup
¼ tsp each of salt & pepper
¼ tsp ajinomoto (optional)
¼ cup chicken stock
2 tbsp oil

1. Mix all the ingredients of the egg batter. Keep aside.
2. Add 1½ cups water to the chicken pieces and boil for 2-3 minutes in a covered vessel till tender. Strain and wipe dry the pieces. Reserve the stock.
3. Heat oil. Dip the chicken pieces in batter and deep fry the pieces till golden brown. Keep aside.
4. Heat 2 tbsp oil in a wok. Add garlic and green chillies. Stir fry.
5. Reduce flame. Add the soya sauce, tomato ketchup, chilli paste, salt, pepper, ajinomoto and ¼ cup chicken stock.
6. Add the fried chicken pieces and stir fry on high flame till the sauces coat the chicken pieces. Serve hot, garnished with chopped spring onions.

Fried Chicken Wontons

Serves 4

STUFFING
100 gms cooked chicken mince
1 tbsp chopped spring onions
salt to taste
¼ tsp ajinomoto, optional
2 egg whites - beaten

WONTON SHEETS
1 cup flour
2 tbsp cornflour
2 eggs
oil for frying

1. Make a firm dough using flour, cornflour, eggs and just enough water to bind. Keep in a cool place covered with a wet cloth for 30 minutes.
2. Mix all ingredients of the stuffing together.
3. Take out the dough and roll out flat as thin as possible. Cut square sheets 2½" x 2½".
4. Put a little stuffing in the centre and give it a boat shape or a bag shape with the stuffing in the center. Seal the sides using egg.
5. Deep fry in hot oil till golden brown. Drain.
6. Serve hot with tomato ketchup or chilli sauce.

Thai Peanut Corn Cutlets

6-8 cutlets

3/4 cup corn kernels (fresh, tinned or frozen), 3/4 cup roasted peanuts
juice of ½ lemon
1 large potato - boiled and mashed
½ tsp red chilli powder, ½ tsp salt, or to taste, 1½ tsp soya sauce
1 tbsp chopped coriander leaves
4 tbsp cornflour, ½ tsp baking powder

1. Grind corn and peanuts in the mixer with lemon juice to a rough paste.
2. Mix all other ingredients. Add the corn and peanut paste. Mix well.
3. Shape into cutlets and deep fry.

Fish Milanese

Serves 4-6

Italian fried fish with parsley garlic butter. You would never have tasted such delicious fish.

500 gms fish fillet (6 large pieces, preferably skinless & boneless)

MARINADE
1 onions - minced or grated fine
4 tbsp lemon juice
1½ tsp salt
1½ tsp pepper
4 tbsp oil

OTHER INGREDIENT
1 egg
1 tbsp milk
½ tsp salt, ½ tsp pepper
some bread crumbs
some flour (maida) for coating fish
oil for frying

INGREDIENT FOR PARSLEY GARLIC BUTTER
4 tbsp butter
4 cloves garlic - crushed
4 tbsp parsley or coriander chopped fine

1. Mix all ingredients of the marinade together & marinate the fish in it 1-2 hours.
2. Beat egg, milk, salt & pepper lightly together.
3. Heat oil in a frying pan.
4. Dip or coat fish pieces lightly with flour.
5. Dip them in egg mixture and now roll them up in bread crumbs.
6. Deep fry to a golden brown. Place on serving dish.
7. To prepare the butter, heat butter add garlic.
8. Fry for 1 minute and add parsley. Mix well and pour a little over each piece of fish.
9. Serve immediately garnished with sprigs of parsley.

Note: This can be served as a snack or as the main use with a salad and steamed vegetables tossed in butter with some garlic.

Suppli

Gives 12 large balls   *Picture on cover*

An Italian cheesy snack with a saffron flavour.

1 onion - finely chopped
4 tbsp butter
1 cup rice (raw)
a few strands of saffron or ½ tsp powdered saffron
1 tsp salt
1 tsp pepper
2 tbsp chopped fresh parsely or coriander
1 tbsp grated cheese (parmesan or mozzarella)
2 eggs
75 gm mozzarella cheese - cut into ¼" cubes
bread crumbs to coat

1. Heat 2 tbsp butter. Add chopped onion. Fry for 1-2 minutes.
2. Add washed rice. Fry for 1-2 minutes.
3. Add saffron, salt & pepper.
4. Add 2½ cups water. Boil. Cover and cook on low heat till all the water is absorbed and rice is cooked. Cook further for 2 more minutes and dry the rice completely. Remove from fire.
5. Add parsely/dhania, 2 tbsp butter and 1 tbsp grated cheese. Mix and let the mixture cool.
6. Beat eggs lightly and mix carefully with the rice.
7. Cut mozzarella cheese into small cubes or grate it.
8. Divide the rice mixture into 12 equal portions. Make a ball with one portion. Flatten it. Place some grated cheese or 1-2 cubes of cheese inside and cover completely with rice mixture. Shape into a large round or oblong balls, like the shape of an egg.
9. Roll over dry bread crumbs and keep aside in the refrigerator. Do with all the rice mixture.
10. At serving time, deep fry to a golden brown colour. Serve hot.

VARIATION

• A small piece of ham can be added along with the grated or cubed cheese for ham suppli.
• Left over rice or risotto can be used to make suppli.
• Can have plain suppli by omitting the saffron.

Penne with Basil

Serves 4-6   *Picture on facing page*

2 tbsp olive oil or butter
1 onion - finely chopped
2 garlic flakes - crushed
500 gm tomatoes - blanched in hot water, skinned & pureed till smooth
1 tsp dried oregano
1 tbsp tomato sauce
2 tbsp chopped fresh basil or mint or parsely
½ tsp sugar, 1 tsp salt, or to taste
3 cups boiled penne or any other pasta (boil 2 cups raw pasta)
½ cup grated cheese (mozerella) to sprinkle on top
some freshly ground pepper
a few basil leaves - put in chilled water to garnish

1. Heat oil. Add onion & garlic, cook until onions turn light brown.
2. Add tomatoes, oregano, tomato sauce, basil, salt and sugar, cook for 5 minutes, stirring occasionally. Keep sauce aside.
3. At serving time, melt 1 tbsp butter in a non stick and toss the pasta in it. Sprinkle a pinch of salt and some pepper on it and mix till it's heated. Remove from fire.
4. Heat the prepared tomato sauce. Add pasta and heat through. Transfer to a serving dish.
5. Serve sprinkled with grated cheese and basil leaves.

COCKTAIL

Snacks

Baby Corn Niblers

Serves 6-8

4 bread slices

TOPPING
100 gm baby corn
2-3 laung (cloves)
1½ tbsp butter
2 tbsp maida
1 cup milk
2 tbsp grated cheese or cheese spread
1 tsp chopped fresh parsley or ½ tsp dried basil
salt to taste
5-6 drops Tabasco sauce or a pinch of red chilli powder
black or green grapes cut into halves, for garnishing

1. Boil 2 cups water with a little salt, ¼ tsp haldi and 2-3 cloves (laung). Add baby corns and boil for 2 minutes. Remove and cut into thin round slices.
2. To prepare the topping, heat butter in a pan.
3. Add maida. Cook till slightly brown, remove from heat.
4. Gradually add the milk, stirring continuously, so that no lump forms.
5. Return the pan to heat. Cook, stirring continuously, till the sauce thickens and starts leaving the sides of the pan. Remove from heat.
6. Add baby corn, cheese, salt, tabasco sauce, parsley or basil.
7. Spread baby corn spread on bread slices.
8. Grill bread in a hot oven at 210°C for 8-10 minutes, till the under side turns crisp.
9. Cut into 4 squares or triangles.
10. Garnish each piece with a halved black or green grape.

Broccoli Balls

Serves 8

200 gm broccoli (1 small head) - chopped finely along with tender stalks (1½ cups chopped)
1 onion - chopped finely
1 tbsp butter

SAUCE
3 tbsp melted butter
4 tbsp maida (plain flour)
1 cup milk
¼ tsp each salt & pepper, or to taste

COATING
½ cup maida mixed with ½ cup water or 1 egg white
1 cup bread crumbs
oil for frying

1. Chop the broccoli florest and the tender stems very finely.
2. Heat butter in a pan. Add chopped onion. Stir and add the chopped broccoli. Add 2 pinches of salt. Cook on medium heat for about 2-3 minutes on low heat, till slightly tender. Remove from heat.
3. To prepare the sauce, heat butter in a clean pan. Add maida and cook till maida turns slightly brown.
4. Remove from heat and add milk, stirring continuously. Return to heat. Cook till the sauce thickens and start leaving the sides of the pan.
5. Add salt, pepper and cooked broccoli. Cook further for 1-2 minutes on low heat. Remove from heat. Cool well.
6. Slightly wet your hands and make balls of the cold broccoli mixture. If the mixture is even slightly warm, it becomes difficult to make balls. Keep in the refrigerator till serving time.
7. Prepare the coating mixture by mixing maida and water or use egg white mixed with 2 tbsp water.
8. Heat oil in a kadhai.
9. Dip in the coating mixture or egg white and roll in bread crumbs. Fry til golden brown. Drain on absorbent paper. Serve.

Fish Fingers with Tartar Sauce

Serves 6-8

½ kg firm white fish fillet (Sole), without bones - cut into fingers
3/4 cup dry bread crumbs for coating

MARINADE
1 tbsp ginger paste
½ tsp salt, ½ tsp pepper powder, ½ tsp red chilli powder
½ tsp mustard paste
1 tsp tomato sauce
1 egg white
a few coriander leaves - chopped

TARTAR SAUCE
½ cup mayonnaise
1 tbsp very finely chopped cucumber
1 tbsp very finely chopped onion
1 tbsp chopped coriander or parsley
2 tbsp brown vinegar

1. Rub a little lemon juice on the fish fingers and wash the fish well. Transfer them to a kitchen towel and pat till well dried.
2. To prepare the marinade, mix all the ingredients together in a small bowl.
3. Transfer the fish to a flat plate and rub the marinade on the fish. Keep aside for ½ hour.
4. Press the fish fingers on the bread crumbs such that they coat the fish. Fry on medium heat. Drain on absorbent paper. Serve hot.
5. To prepare the tartar sauce, soak the onion and cucumber in vinegar for 10-15 minutes.
6. Strain the cucumber and onion in vinegar to drain out the vinegar. Press gently to remove any excess vinegar.
7. Gently mix it into the mayonnaise. Serve with fish fingers.

Italian Dill Canapes

Serves 8-10

4-5 slices of wheat bread
¼ cup thick curd - hang for 30 minutes in a muslin cloth
1-2 tsp dried dill (soye) flakes or coriander chopped
1 small cucumber - cut into paper thin slices without peeling
1 cube cheese - grated or 2 tbsp cheese spread

ITALIAN SPREAD
½ onion - chopped, 2 flakes garlic - chopped
1 tbsp oil, 1 tsp vinegar (white)
¼ tsp ajwain or ½ tsp oregano, ¼ tsp red chilli powder, ½ tsp salt, ¼ tsp sugar

1. Blend all ingredients of the paste along with hung curd in a grinder for 3-4 minutes till smooth. Remove from blender and add cheese. Check salt.
2. Toast slices slightly. Cut each slice into 4 squares. Spread 1 tbsp of spread on each piece. Press a cucumber slice, projecting outside, a little away from the center towards the corner with the crust & sprinkle dill.

Note: Dry fresh soye in the microwave to get green, dried and flaky dill.

Crunchy Rolls

18-20 pieces

1 cup dalia (cracked wheat)
150 gm (1 cup mashed) paneer (cottage cheese)
1 tsp salt, ½ tsp red chilli powder
2-3 green chillies - chopped fine
½" piece ginger - chopped fine
1 tsp dhania (coriander) powder
1 tsp garam masala, 1 tsp amchoor (dry mango powder)
2-3 tbsp chopped coriander leaves
1 tsp lemon juice
oil for frying

1. Soak dalia in water for 1 hour. Strain. Squeeze out excess water by pressing well in the strainer.
2. Mix crumbled paneer and all other ingredients to the dalia. Mix well.
3. Form into 1" long rolls & deep fry 1 or 2 pieces at a time in hot oil till golden brown. Serve hot with soups.

Vegetable & Cheese Dumplings

Serves 8

2 cups (250 gms) roughly chopped ghiya (bottle gourd)
2 slices of bread
3/4 cup finely grated carrot (1 carrot)
3/4 cup grated cabbage
¼ cup mashed paneer
1 tsp salt
½ tsp pepper or to taste
¼ tsp each of amchoor, red chilli powder and garam masala
2 tbsp bread crumbs and some more to coast
50 gm mozzarella cheese - cut into ¼" cubes
oil for frying

1   Pressure cook peeled and chopped ghiya with 1 tbsp water to give 1 whistle. Remove from fire and put under running water to let the pressure drop. Transfer to a plate and let it cool down.

2. Mix grated carrot, cabbage, paneer, salt, pepper, amchoor, garam masala red chilli powder and 2 tbsp bread crumbs.

3. Break the bread slices roughly and put in a blender. Grind for a few seconds to get fresh bread crumbs. Drain the steamed ghiya. Add the drained ghiya and churn to grind the ghiya alongwith the bread in the blender to a paste.

4. Add the ghiya paste to the carrot mixture and mix well. If the mixture feels too soft to form into balls, churn some more bread in the mixer to form crumbs and add to the ghiya mixture.

5. Make balls, flatten a little and stuff 1 small piece of cheese inside. Make a ball again. Roll in bread crumbs scattered in a plate.

6. Deep fry 1-2 pieces at a time, on medium heat till golden. Drain on paper napkins.

7. Arrange in a serving plate sprinkled with some shredded carrots and cabbage. Finely grate some cheese on the dumplings.

8. Serve with a spicy tomato ketchup as an evening snack or as a starter before the main meals.

Cheesy Paneer Bites

Serves 4

1½ tbsp butter
4 slices brown or white bread
1 tsp garlic (5-6 flakes) - crushed and chopped
100 gms (25-30) leaves of paalak (spinach) - washed & shredded
150 gms paneer (cottage cheese) - grated
1 tbsp basil or coriander - chopped
5 tbsp mozzarella cheese (Amul) - grated
¼ tsp salt and pepper, or to taste
some red chilli flakes

1. Wash and shred the spinach leaves into thin ribbons. Pat dry on a kitcnen towel.
2. Heat butter in a kadhai or pan.
3. Add garlic and stir. Add the spinach and cook till all the moisture of the spinach evaporates. Remove from heat.
4. Mix grated paneer, basil or coriander and 4 tbsp grated mozzarella cheese, leaving behind 1 tbsp for the topping.
5. Add cooked spinach to the paneer and mix well. Add salt and pepper.
6. Toast the slices and spread the mixture on the toasts. Sprinkle some mozzarella cheese. Sprinkle some red chilli flakes too.
7. Grill in the oven (210°C) for 2-3 minutes and serve hot cut into triangles or squares.

Stuffed Potato Shells

Serves 4-5

4 oblong potatoes - medium size

FILLING
50-75 gm paneer - crumbled
¼ tsp roasted powdered jeera (bhuna jeera)
½ tsp tandoori masala
1 tbsp chopped mint (poodina)
1 tsp lemon juice
1 tbsp oil
salt to taste
chat masala to sprinkle
oil for frying

1. Boil the potatoes (pressure cook to give 1 whistle) or microwave in a polythene bag (sprinkle little water) for 5 minutes, till slightly tender.
2. Peel and slice the potatoes lengthwise into two halves. Scope out the potatoes to get a hollow with a tiny scupper or a small coffee spoon. Make the outer shell quite thin.
3. Heat oil in a kadhai and deep fry the potato shells on medium heat till light brown and crisp. Drain. Sprinkle chat masala on the potato shells. Keep aside.
4. For the filling, mix all the ingredients of the filling and fill the hollow potato shells. Press the filling.
5. At the time of serving, heat oven to 210° C and grill the potatoes for 3-4 minutes, just enough to heat.
6. Cut each potato piece into half lengthways and serve.

Minty Mutton Kababs

Makes 15 kababs   *Picture on facing page*

PRESSURE COOK TOGETHER
½ kg mutton mince (keema)
¼ cup channa dal - soaked & drained
1 onion - sliced
10 flakes garlic - chopped, 2" piece ginger - chopped
2 tsp saboot dhania (coriander seeds)
1 tsp jeera (cumin seeds), 3-4 laung (cloves)
2 chhoti illaichi (green cardamoms)
2 moti illaichi (brown cardamoms)
½" stick dalchini (cinnamon), 1 bay leaf
4-5 saboot kali mirch (peppercorns)
2-3 dry, whole red chillies
salt to taste
½ cup water

MINTY FILLING (MIX TOGETHER)
1 onion - finely chopped
1 tbsp chopped pudina, 1 tbsp chopped hara dhania
2 green chillies - finely chopped

1. Wash the mince and drain out the water well through a strainer. Press well to squeeze out all the water.
2. Add all the ingredients to the mince and pressure cook to give 2 whistles. Keep on low flame for 2 minutes. Remove from fire.
3. When the pressure drops, uncover the pressure cooker. If there is any water left, keep the cooker on fire to dry the water. (If the mince is wet, the kebabs will break while frying).
4. Dry grind the well dried minced meat either on a stone grinder or in a mixer till smooth without adding any water while grinding. (Discard hard residue of moti illaichi & bay leaf)
5. To prepare the kababs, make 2 tiny balls. Flatten both and sandwich them together with a teaspoon of the filling mixture. Press gently to stick together.
6. Shallow fry in a little oil on a non stick tawa on medium heat, till brown.

Minty Mutton Kababs ➢
Drums of Heaven: Recipe on page 65 ➢

Garlic Mushroom Supremo

Serves 4-6

long garlic bread loaf - cut diagonally into ¼" thick slices (8 slices)
2 tbsp softened butter
1 tsp basil (dried) or ½ tsp saboot kali mirch (peppercorns) - crushed
1 tbsp finely chopped coriander or parsley
2 flakes garlic - crushed
6 mushrooms - cut into paper thin slices
75 gm pizza cheese (mozzeralla) - grated
1 tomato - cut into slices

1. Cut the garlic bread into moderately thick slices diagonally.
2. Mix the butter, basil, coriander & garlic.
3. Apply this butter lightly on the bread slice.
4. Arrange mushroom slices on the buttered slices. Sprinkle grated cheese on them.
5. Place a slice of tomato on it and put 2-3 shreds of cheese on it also.
6. Heat oven to 210°C. Place the grill rack in the center of the oven and grill the slices (7-8 minutes) till slightly crisp and toasted. Serve hot whole or cut into two halves.

Corn Vegetable Hearts

Makes 4-5

½ cup suji (semolina)
1 cup milk
¼ cup paneer (cottage cheese)-mashed
1 tbsp butter
3/4 cup finely diced mixed vegetables (4-6 beans, 1 small carrot, ¼ cup chopped cabbage)
1/3 cup cooked corn kernels (fresh or tinned)
¼ cup coriander leaves - chopped
2 green chillies - chopped finely
salt to taste
¼ tsp garam masala, ½ tsp red chilli flakes, ½ tsp chaat masala
2 tsp lemon juice, 1 tsp tomato sauce

COATING
bread crumbs
2 tbsp maida dissolved in ¼ cup water to get a thin maida batter
oil for frying

1. Heat butter in a kadhai. Add very finely chopped vegetables and ¼ tsp salt. Saute for 2-3 minutes. Cover and keep on low heat for 1-2 minutes till cooked. Keep vegetables aside.
2. Add suji and stir fry on low heat for 2-3 minutes.
3. Add milk, stirring continuously. Cook till thick. Keep on low flame for 1-2 minutes more, stirring constantly, until dry and forms a lump
4. Add corn, paneer and coriander. Mix well.
5. Remove from fire. Transfer to a paraat. Add all other ingredients except the coating ingredients. Mix very well. Check seasonings.
6. Make small heart shaped cutlets with greased or wet hands. Dip them in maida batter. Roll in bread crumbs spread on a plate.
7. Deep fry 1-2 pieces at a time.

TiP: To make crisper cutlets keep them in the fridge, for 15-20 minutes before frying, to set them well.

Flaming Mushrooms

Serves 12

100 gm small sized mushrooms, about 12-14 pieces
1 capsicum - cut into thin long fingers
3-4 flakes garlic - crushed
1½ tsp soya sauce
1 tbsp vinegar
½ tbsp chilli sauce (red)
1 tbsp tomato ketchup
¼ tsp salt and ¼ tsp pepper, or to taste
1½ tbsp oil
tooth picks

BATTER
3 tbsp cornflour
2 tbsp maida
4-6 flakes garlic - crushed
1 tbsp hot oil
1 tsp soya sauce, 1 tsp vinegar
1/3 tsp salt, 1/3 tsp pepper
a big pinch of ajinomoto, optional
¼ tsp baking powder
3-4 tbsp water

1. Mix all ingredients of the batter and add water with a spoon to see that it remains thick and of a good coating consistency. Keep aside for 5-7 minutes.
2. Wash and trim the stem of mushrooms. Wipe dry on a clean kitchen towel. Cut the long strips of capsicum into 2 halves to get 1" long pieces.
3. Dip the mushrooms in maida batter and deep fry in 2 batches till golden. Keep aside.
4. Heat 2 tbsp oil in a nonstick pan. Reduce heat. Add garlic. Let it turn light brown.
5. Remove from fire. Add soya sauce, vinegar, tomato sauce and chilli sauce, salt and pepper. Return to fire and cook the sauces on low heat for ½ minute.
6. Add capsicum. Stir for 1-2 minutes.
7. Add fried mushrooms and mix well for 1 minute. Do not keep on fire for long. Remove from fire.
8. Thread a mushroom, then a capsicum and again a mushroom on each tooth pick. Serve.

Pan Fried Paneer Tikka

Serves 8-12

500 gms paneer - cut into 1½" squares of ½" thickness
2-3 tbsp oil
2 capsicums - cut into 3/4" cubes

MARINADE
¼ cup thick curd - hung to drain the water
4 tbsp cream
1 tsp lemon juice, 1 tsp tandoori masala, ½ tsp chat masala
½ tsp red chilli powder, ½ tsp black salt
a pinch of haldi, salt to taste

1. Mix hung curd with all the other ingredients of the marinade and marinate paneer with it. Keep aside in the fridge till serving time.
2. At the time of serving, heat a non stick tawa. Spread 2 tbsp oil on the tawa. Place the marinated paneer pieces one by one on the tawa (they should not overlap). Cook on both sides for 1-2 minutes till masala slightly coasts the paneer pieces (over cooking hardens paneer). Remove on to a serving platter.
3. Toss capsicum cubes on the tawa. Saute and sprinkle chaat masala.
4. Place one capsicum cube on each paneer piece. Pierce both with a toothpick and serve hot.

Nutty Paneer Balls

Serves 8

4 slices bread - remove sides
6 tbsp curd
200 gms paneer - mashed, ¼ tsp baking powder
2 green chillies - finely chopped, 2 tbsp finely chopped green coriander
1 tsp salt and ½ tsp pepper, or to taste
3 tbsp maida, a few pieces of cashewnuts

1. Spread 3/4 tbsp curd on each side of each slice of bread, to wet it. After spreading curd on both sides of the bread, keep aside for a minute.
2. Mash the paneer well. Add baking powder, green chillies and coriander.
3. Mash the bread slices well and mix with the paneer. Add salt and pepper.
4. Add maida in the end. Make balls and stuff a piece of cashew in the centre.
5. Deep fry in medium hot oil. Serve with tomato sauce or mint chutney.

Ham & Cheese Dream

Serves 4-6

8 slices bread
4 slices cheese, 4 slices ham
2 tsp mustard paste (optional)
2 tbsp butter, or enough to butter the slices

1. Butter bread slices on one side.
2. Place a slice of cheese on the unbuttered side, keeping the buttered side outside.
3. Spread a little mustard paste. Cover the cheese slice with a ham slice and place another bread slice over the ham slice with the buttered side outside.
4. Repeat this with other slices to get 4 sandwiches.
5. Heat oven on 200°C. Place the grill rack in the center of the oven and grill the sandwich for 10 minutes or till crisp and golden or toast sandwiches on both side in a non stick pan or a sandwich toaster.
6. Cut diagonally and serve hot with ketchup.

Egg Kababs

Serves 4-6

4 eggs - hard boiled
2 tbsp besan (gram flour)
1 onion - chopped finely, 2-3 green chillies - chopped finely
1 tbsp poodina - chopped finely, 1 tbsp hara dhania - chopped finely
½ tsp garam masala, a few drops of lemon juice
salt to taste, oil for shallow frying

1. Grate the hard boiled eggs finely.
2. Add chopped onions, green chillies, poodina, dhania, besan, garam masala, lemon juice & salt. Mix well to make a smooth dough.
3. Shape into small flat kebabs (10-12). Keep aside.
4. At the time of serving, heat oil in a shallow frying pan. Add 3-4 kebabs at a time. Fry on moderate heat till golden. Remove on absorbent paper.
5. Garnish with onion rings and chopped mint. Sprinkle chat masala. Serve with mint chutney.

Vegetarian Shami Kebabs

Servings 12

BOIL TOGETHER
½ cup kale channe (black gram)
1 tbsp channe ki dal (split gram)
¼ tsp jeera (cumin seeds)
1" stick dalchini (cinnamon)
3-4 laung (cloves)
3-4 saboot kali mirch (pepper corns)
2 flakes garlic - optional
½" piece ginger
1 dry, red chilli
1 onion - chopped
2 slices bread - dipped in water and squeezed
¼ tsp amchoor (dry mango powder)
salt to taste

1. Soak channas and channe ki dal together in about 2½ cups water for 6-8 hours or overnight.
2. Pressure cook channas with jeera, dalchini, moti illaichi, laung, kali mirch, garlic, onion & red chilli to give one whistle. Keep on low heat for 20 minutes.
3. If these is any water left, dry the channas on fire, leaving just a little water which is enough to grind.
4. Grind to a fine paste. Add bread, salt and amchoor to taste.
5. Chill the mixture in the fridge for sometime.
6. Make small flattened rounds.
7. Deep fry 4-5 pieces in medium hot oil. Drain on absorbent paper.
8. Sprinkle onion rings over the kababs. Garnish with chopped poodina leaves. Serve with yoghurt minty dip as given on page 113.

Note: If the kebabs break on frying, add 1-2 tbsp of maida or an egg white to the mixture.

Chicken Nuggets

Serves 4

4 chicken (broiler) thighs - each cut into 2 pieces
2 tbsp lemon juice
4-5 flakes garlic - crushed
¼ tsp freshly ground pepper
salt to taste

COATING
¼ cup maida - seasoned with little salt
1 egg - beaten with little water
½ cup dried bread crumbs
oil for frying

1. Place the chicken pieces in a bowl. Marinate with lemon juice, garlic, salt and pepper for 6-8 hours. Keep in the refrigerator.
2. Keep maida in a plate. Beat egg in a bowl. Keep bread crumbs in a shallow plate.
3. Coat each chicken piece well with maida (press well in maida). Dip in egg and press in bread crumbs. Refrigerate till frying.
4. Heat oil on medium heat.
5. Deep fry on low heat for 3-4 minutes, 2-3 at a time, till golden brown and chicken is cooked. Drain on absorbent paper.
6. Garnish with lemon wedges and a coriander or parsley sprig. Serve hot with sauce.

Note: If very soft chicken is desired, you can pressure cook chicken pieces to 2 whistles by adding ½ cup water after marination. Drain the water from the pieces well and dip the pieces in flour first, then in egg and finally in crumbs and fry.

Chunky Chicken Canapes

Serves 4-6

10-12 monnacco or any salted biscuits
1 chicken breast - boiled and flaked
½ cup thick mayonnaise, 2 tbsp cream
8-10 almonds - blanched (skinned) & chopped
1 tsp lemon juice
salt and pepper to taste

FOR GARNISHING
cherry, pineapple, grapes or oranges

1. In a bowl, mix chicken, mayonnaise, cream, lemon juice, almonds, salt and pepper. Keep aside till serving time.
2. At serving time, spoon chicken mixture on each biscuit.
3. Garnish each canape with pineapple, grapes, cherry or orange. Serve cold.

Grilled Chilli Prawns

Serves 5-6

10-12 medium size prawns
3-4 flakes garlic - crushed & chopped finely
½ tsp red chilli flakes, ½ tsp salt, ½ tsp sugar
2 tbsp lemon juice, 1 tbsp chopped coriander
1 tbsp oil
salt to taste

1. Wash and devein the prawns. Pat dry.
2. Mix all the ingredients in a bowl. Add the prawns coating them well. Cover and leave to marinate the prawns in it for 1 hour.
3. Arrange the marinated prawns on a baking tray. Bake in a hot oven at 200°C for 10-12 minutes, basting with oil in between.
4. Serve atonce, garnished with lemon wedges and fresh coriander.

Note: Be particular about the baking time, do not over bake.

Peshawari Murg Tikka

Serves 4   *Picture on facing page*

2-3 breasts of chicken (broiler), boneless - cut into 2" pieces (8-12 pieces)
some chat masala, lemon juice and coriander leaves

1ST MARINADE
2 tbsp malt vinegar or lemon juice
¼ tsp salt
½ tsp chilli powder

2ND MARINADE
1/3 cup thick hung curd (hang about 3/4 cup curd)
2 tsp ginger-garlic paste
2-3 tbsp thick malai or cream
¼ tsp black salt, ½ tsp garam masala powder
¼ tsp red chilli powder, salt to taste
2-3 drops of red colour
butter to baste

1. Wash the chicken pieces and pat dry on a kitchen towel.
2. Marinate the pieces in the 1st marinade for ½ hour.
3. In a bowl mix curd, cream, ginger-garlic paste, black salt, garam masala, red chilli powder, colour and salt to taste.
4. Remove the chicken pieces from the 1st marinade. Pat dry slightly. Add to the curd mixture and marinate for 6-8 hours. Keep in the refrigerator.
5. Heat a gas tandoor on gas or an electric oven at 200°C. Place the well coated chicken pieces on the grill or skewer the chicken pieces. Roast for 8-10 minutes or until cooked, thoroughly basting with butter or oil at least once in between.
6. Sprinkle with chat masala and lemon juice.
7. Serve hot garnished onion rings and coriander leaves.

Galouti Kebabs

Serves 8-10

500 gm keema (lamb mince)
2 onions - cut into slices
2 tbsp ginger-garlic paste
2 tbsp besan (gram flour)
1 egg
1 tsp garam masala
½ tsp red chilli powder
salt to taste
oil for frying

1. Place the mince in a strainer and squeeze out excess water.
2. Heat 1 cup oil in a kadhai and fry the onions till golden brown. Remove from oil with a slotted spoon and grind to paste.
3. Place the mince in a mixer blender. Add the brown onion paste, ginger-garlic paste, egg, salt, chilli and garam masala. Blend to get a sticky consistency. Remove in a bowl.
4. Heat a non stick pan. Add the besan and roast on medium heat till the light brown.
5. Add roasted besan to the mince mixture. Add the chopped coriander also. Keep aside for 1-2 hours or till frying.
6. Heat oil in a shallow pan. Shape the mince into flat tikkis. Shallow fry on medium heat till brown on both sides.
7. Garnish with onion rings and a mint sprig.

Golden Fried Prawns

Serves 4

Sprinkle sesame seeds for the exotic look

(250 gms) 12 large prawns - cleaned & deveined

MARINADE
1 tbsp soya sauce
1 tbsp wine or sherry, optional
¼ tsp ajionomoto
½ tsp salt, ¼ tsp pepper

BATTER
1 egg
3 tbsp flour, 3 tbsp cornflour
¼ tsp baking powder
¼ tsp white pepper
¼ tsp salt, ¼ tsp ajinomoto, optional
1 tbsp oil
1 tbsp sesame seeds

1. In a bowl mix soya sauce, sherry, ajinomoto, salt and pepper and marinate the prawns for 15-30 minutes.
2. Make a smooth paste by adding flour, cornflour, baking powder, oil, salt, pepper and ajinomoto to egg. Add just enough water to get a very thick batter such that it coats well.
3. Dip the prawns into the batter.
4. Sprinkles sesame seeds and deep fry one to two pieces at a time, till golden brown.
5. Serve hot with chilli sauce.

Note: If desired you can let the tail remain and then marinate the prawns.

DIPS & CHUTNEYS

To serve with Snacks

Serve these unusual dips with crunchy & crisp carrot and cucumber cut into thin long fingers as starters for the calorie conscious! Even fruit slices like apple pieces taste good with these dips. Remember to chill the vegetable and fruit sticks well in advance. For the carefree ones, keep some cheese crackers biscuits, potato fingers, nacho chips or potato wafers along with the vegetable and fruit sticks.

Fresh curd should be used to prepare the yogurt dips. Tie the thick curd in a muslin cloth and hang for an hour to drain out the liquid. About 1 cup of thick curd when hung gives about ½ cup hung curd. The sourness also lessens when the whey (the liquid) is drained away from the curd. So, the curd is hung got not only to make it thick but also to reduce the sourness of a yogurt dip.

Yogurt Minty Dip

Serves 6   *Picture on back cover*

1 cup thick fresh curd
1 tsp oil
a pinch of kala namak (rock salt)
2 tbsp paste of coriander and mint leaves or green chutney
½ tsp powdered sugar
salt, pepper to taste
a drop of green colour

1. Beat curd well till smooth.
2. Add all other ingredients. A little colour must be added to get the bright green colour..

Instant Khatti Mithi Chutney

Serves 6

1 tbsp amchoor (dried mango powder)
3 tbsp sugar or shakkar (gur)
½ tsp roasted jeera (cumin seeds) powder
¼ tsp red chilli powder
¼ tsp salt
¼ tsp garam masala
¼ cup water

1. Mix all ingredients together in a small heavy bottomed pan.
2. Cook on low flame, till all the ingredients dissolve properly and the chutney the right consistency.
3. Cool. Serve with Indian snacks.

Orange Yogurt Dip

Serves 8

**3 cups thick yogurt - hung for 1 hour to give 1½ cups hung curd
2 tbsp tomato puree (ready made)
3 tbsp orange juice (ready made)
1 tsp lemon juice
1 tsp lemon rind - grate only the peel of whole lemon gently on the grater
1 tbsp vinegar
1 tsp red chilli paste
salt & sugar to taste**

1. Mix all the ingredients of yogurt dip and blend well till smooth. Refrigerate till serving time.
2. To serve, put yogurt dip in a bowl and place it on a serving plate. Arrange chips, cream crackers or fruits and vegetable sticks all around it. Serve cold.

Strawberry Mint Dip

Serves 8

**3 cups curd - hung in a muslin cloth for 1 hour
3/4 cup chopped strawberries
¼ cup chopped mint
¼ tsp sugar
salt to taste**

**TO SERVE WITH
vegetable sticks of carrots, cucumber or blanched broccoli florest**

1. Tie the yogurt in a muslin cloth and hang it to drain for 1 hour. 3 cups yogurt will give about 1½ cups hung yogurt.
2. Blend strawberries for a few seconds to make a strawberry puree.
3. Beat the yogurt till smooth.
4. Mix strawberry puree, mint, salt & sugar. Chill.
5. Serve with peeled carrot and cucumber cut into sticks and blanched broccoli florest.

Salsa

4 (medium) tomatoes
2 onion - chopped
2-3 green chillies - chopped
2 tbsp chopped green coriander
1 tbsp oil
salt & white pepper to taste
1 tsp vinegar

1. Pierce the tomato with a fork. Hold it over the flame with the fork and roast it on all sides till slightly charred. Repeat with all the tomatoes.
2. Cool and peel. Chop 2 tomatoes and puree the other 2.
3. Heat oil in a pan. Add onions and green chillies. Stir and add the chopped tomatoes and the pureed tomatoes, salt, pepper, vinegar and coriander. Remove from heat (salsa does not require too much cooking, just mix over heat and remove quickly). Serve with nacho chips.

Nutty Dip

Serves 8

1 cup mayonnaise
¼ cup of coarsely powdered nuts (walnuts, almonds, peanuts or cashew nuts)
a few raisins (kishmish)
3-4 flakes garlic - crushed & chopped
2 tsp lemon juice
2 tbsp chopped parsley or coriander

1. Add all the ingredients to mayonnaise. Mix well to blend.
2. Chill and serve with crisp carrot & cucumber sticks, French fries or nacho chips.

Poodina Chutney

Serves 6

½ cup poodina leaves (½ bunch)
1 cup hara dhania (coriander) chopped along with stem
2 green chillies
1 onion - chopped
1½ tsp amchoor (dried mango pd.)
1½ tsp sugar
½ tsp salt

1. Wash coriander and mint leaves.
2. Grind all ingredients with just enough water to get the right chutney consistency.

Coconut Chutney

Serves 6

½ cup freshly grated or desiccated (dry pd.) coconut
¼ cup roasted channa or channe ki dal (split gram) - roasted
1 green chilli - chopped
1 onion - chopped
3/4 tsp salt
¼" piece ginger
1 cup sour curd - approx.

BAGHAR
1 tbsp oil
1 tsp sarson (mustard seeds)
1-2 dry red chillies - broken into bits

1. Grind all ingredients of the chutney adding enough curd to get the right consistency. Keep aside in a bowl.
2. Heat 1 tbsp oil. Add sarson. When it splutters, add broken red chillies.
3. Pour the baghar into the chutney. Serve with South Indian snacks.

SWEET
Snacks

Although mithai, cakes and pastries are very easily available but the joy and satisfaction you get by making these yourself is beyond compare. These can be prepared a day or two in advance too so that you can devote all your time and attention to the other snacks on the day of the party. Enjoy them with tea or as desserts!

Chocolate Sandesh

Serves 10

1 kg milk
juice of 1 lemon
2 tbsp cocoa powder
10 tbsp powdered sugar
a pinch of chhoti illaichi (green cardamom) powder
a few almonds - cut into halves, for garnishing

1. Boil milk. Add lemon juice only after the milk boils. Stir till it curdles. Add a little more lemon juice if it does not curdle properly. See that the green water (whey) separates.
2. Strain the chhena through a muslin cloth. Dip the chhena tied in the cloth in ice cold water for 10 minutes. Hang for 15 minutes or more to drain out the whey (liquid). Squeeze liquid, if any.
3. Put chhena in a blender. Add cocoa powder, sugar and cardamom powder and blend till smooth.
4. Remove from blender and transfer to a heavy bottomed kadhai. Cook for 3-4 minutes till the chhena turns dry and becomes semi thick.
5. Grease tiny biscuit moulds. Put an almond half, white side (cut) down.
    Fill with mixture and press well. Invert on to a serving plate.
6. Keep in the fridge till serving time.

Open Paneer Rolls : Recipe on page 31 ➢
Spaghetti & Corn Balls : Recipe on page 76 ➢

Lemon Tarts

Makes 10   *Picture on back cover*

SHORT CRUST PASTRY (DOUGH) FOR TART SHELLS
200 gm maida (plain flour), 100 gm salted butter - cold
a big pinch (1/8 tsp) baking powder, 2 tbsp powdered sugar
3-4 tbsp ice cold water

LEMON FILLING
½ cup lemon juice (juice of 4 lemons)
4 tbsp cornflour, 1 cup yellow, salted butter
1¾ cups sugar, 4 egg yolks
a pinch or a drop of yellow colour
2 tsp vanilla essence
some red coloured jam

1. Cut the cold, solid butter into small pieces.
2. Add baking powder, sugar and butter to the maida. Rub the butter into the maida with the finger tips till it resembles bread crumbs.
3. Add 3-4 tbsp cold water. Bind into a dough of rolling consistency. Knead lightly.
4. Roll out large chappati of 1/8" thickness. Cut out small circles with a biscuit cutter or katori, which is slightly bigger than the tart mould and fit them into tart tins. Prick with a fork and bake blind (empty tarts) at 230°C in a hot oven for 9-10 minutes. Remove the tarts from the tin. Cool.
5. For the filling, grate 2 lemons gently on the fine side of the grater to get 1 tbsp lemon rind. Grate gently to prevent the white part (pith) from being grated as it is bitter. Squeeze ½ cup juice from the lemons and keep aside.
6. In a saucepan, mix cornflour, lemon peel and juice until smooth. Add butter and sugar. Heat to boiling over medium heat. Boil for 1 minute, stirring constantly. Remove from fire. Keep aside.
7. In small bowl, beat egg yolks lightly. Add a small amount of hot lemon mixture into the beaten egg yolks and mix well immediately. Transfer the egg mixture into the lemon mixture in the saucepan, beating rapidly. Keep on very low heat, stirring constantly for about 2-3 minutes, or until thick (do not boil). Remove from fire.
8. Add a pinch colour and essence. Press plastic wrap onto surface to keep skin from forming as it cools. Cool to room temperature.
9. Put 1 tsp jam in the empty tart shell.
10. Put the cooled lemon filling in an icing gun or bag and pipe over the jam in the tart shell to fill the tart shell. Decorate with a dot of jam or a glace cherry.

Choco Truffle Tarts

Makes 10   *Picture on back cover*

3-4 tbsp chopped walnuts

SHORT CRUST PASTRY (DOUGH) FOR TART SHELLS
200 gm maida (plain flour)
100 gm salted butter - cold
a big pinch (1/8 tsp) baking powder
2 tbsp powdered sugar
3-4 tbsp ice cold water

CHOCOLATE BUTTER ICING
1½ cups white butter
1½ cups powdered sugar - sifted
½ cup cocoa, can add more if desired
1 tsp vanilla essence

TRUFFLE FILLING
120 gm chocolate (3 slabs) - softened
50 gm (¼ cup) cream

1. Make the tart shells as given for lemon tarts on page 120. Keep aside to cool.
2. To prepare the chocolate butter icing, whip butter till smooth. Mix all the other ingredients and beat till well blended. Transfer to a piping bag and keep in the refrigerator.
3. For the truffle filling, break chocolate slabs into small pieces and melt in a heavy bottomed nonstick pan or in a microwave.
4. When the chocolate melts, add cream on low heat. Cook for 2 minutes, stirring continuously on low heat. You may add the cream on low power if using the microwave. Do not let it boil. Remove from heat and cool to room temperature.
5. To fill the tart shell, pipe chocolate butter icing at the edges, along the tart shell. Drop a spoonful of truffle filling in the centre to fill the empty space. Sprinkle some chopped walnuts on the sides. Refrigerate till serving time.

Nut & Date Cubes

Serves 8

½ tin milkmaid (condensed milk)
½ cup roasted, salted groundnuts - chopped finely
250 gms dates
½ cup oil
1 cup less 1 tbsp (85 gm) maida (plain flour)
½ tsp vanilla essence
1 tsp baking powder
½ tsp soda-bicarb

1   Remove seeds from dates and chop them finely. Soak in 5 tbsp of water with ½ tsp soda-bicarb for 4-5 hours or overnight or soak in hot water with soda bicarb for 1 hour, if you do not have so much time.
2. Sift maida with baking powder. Transfer to a bowl.
3. Mix dates and groundnuts with the maida.
4. Beat oil and condensed milk in a clean pan. Add essence. Mix.
5. Add half of the maida and date mixture to the milk maid and oil mixture. Mix well. Add the rest of the maida. Beat well.
6. Transfer the mixture to a greased 7" x 4" loaf tin.
7. Bake in a preheated oven at 150°C/300°F for 45-50 minutes.
8. Test by inserting a knife in the highest part of the loaf. If it comes out clean, remove loaf from oven.
9. Remove the loaf from the tin after 5-7 minutes.
10. At serving time cut the loaf into half lengthways, and then cut into 1" thick slices to get cubes.

Apple Malpuas

Serves 2-3

Your guests will be pleasantly surprised at this delicious & ingenious variation of the ordinary malpua.

1 large apple - peeled, cored & cut into thin rounds (approx. 10 rounds)
2 tbsp maida (plain flour)
2 tbsp atta (whole wheat flour)
¼ cup and 1-2 tbsp milk
some grated nutmeg
some cinnamon powder
½ cup sugar
oil for frying

GARNISHING
some grated nutmeg or cinnamon powder
2-3 almonds - blanched and sliced
a little chilled rabri for topping, optional

1   Make batter of maida, atta and milk (use as mucn as needed). The batter should not by very thick or too thin.
2.   Heat oil. Dip apple rounds in batter and fry on high flame to crisp golden brown colour.
3.   Make syrup by boiling ½ cup sugar with slightly less than ½ cup water. After sugar dissolves, keep on low flame for 2-3 minutes only. Remove syrup from heat. (Do not make the syrup very thick).
4.   Dip fried apple rounds in sugar syrup one by one. Leave in the syrup for a few seconds. Remove to a serving plate.
5.   To serve, top malpuas with some chilled rabri or serve warm malpuas sprinkled with nutmeg or cinnamon powder, alongwith cold rabri or ice-cream served separately.
6.   Garnish with blanched almonds.

Orange Cinnamon Slice

Serves 8-10

1¾ cups maida (plain flour)
1½ tsp baking powder
1 cup orange juice
1/3 cup oil
1¼ cups powdered sugar
2 eggs
½ tsp dalchini (cinnamon) powder
4-6 almonds - cut into fine pieces
1-2 tbsp brown sugar

SYRUP
½ cup orange juice
3 tbsp honey
1 tbsp cornflour

1. To prepare the cake, sift maida with baking powder.
2. Beat eggs till stiff in a clean, dry pan.
3. Add sugar gradually and beat well till frothy.
4. Add oil, little at a time and keep beating.
5. Add orange juice and cinnamon powder.
6. Add ½ of the maida and mix gently. Add the left over maida too. Beat well.
7. Transfer to a greased ring mould, (a jelly mould with a hole in the centre.)
8. Sprinkle brown sugar and almonds on top of the cake batter.
8. Bake at 180°C for 30-35 minutes. Bake till a knife inserted in it comes out clean. Cool and remove from tin. Keep aside.
9. Mix all ingredients of the syrup and cook till it attains a coating consistency.
10. Transfer the cake to a serving dish. Prick lightly. Pour the syrup over the cake.
11. Cut into slices and serve.

Nutty Toffee Loaf

Serves 6-8

225 gm seedless dates
½ cup chopped walnuts
½ tsp soda bi-carb
¼ tsp baking powder
85 gm maida (1 cup with 1 tbsp less)
115 gm sugar (3/4 cup)
115 gm white butter
2 eggs
½ tsp vanilla essence

TOFFEE SAUCE
2 tbsp butter
2 tbsp jaggery (powdered gur)
2-3 tbsp fresh cream
1/3 cup chopped walnuts

1. Chop dates. Soak in 5 tbsp water with soda bicarb. Keep aside for 3-4 hours.
2. Sieve flour and baking powder. Mix in the dates.
3. Beat butter and sugar till light and creamy.
4. Add eggs and maida, alternately, beating well. Add essence.
5. Grease and dust 6-8" loaf tin. Pour the mixture in the prepared tin.
6. Bake in a preheated oven at 150°C/300°F for 45-50 minutes. Test by inserting a knife, if it comes out clean, the cake is done. Remove from oven and unmould on a wire rack. Prick the cake slightly for the sauce to seep in. Transfer to the serving platter.
7. To prepare the toffee sauce, heat butter in a small thick bottomed sauce pan on medium heat.
8. Add the jaggery. Cook for ½ minute till the mixture is frothy. Remove from heat.
9. Add the cream. Return to low heat.
10. Stir for a few seconds till well blended. Do not bring to a boil. Add the walnuts.
11. Remove from fire and pour over the cake kept in the serving platter. Spread to get an even coating of the sauce.

Chocolate Truffle Slice

Serves 10-12

Rich Chocolate cake iced with a dark chocolate icing, sliced into wedges and served.

CAKE
4 eggs
1¼ cups powdered sugar
1 cup flour (maida)
½ cup cocoa powder
2 level tsp baking powder
¼ tsp soda-bicarb
1 cup oil
1 tsp vanilla essence

CHOCOLATE ICING
180 gms (1 cup) fresh white butter
1 cup icing sugar - sifted
½ cup cocoa approx.
½ tsp brandy essence or 1 tsp vanilla essence

ICING FOR THE TOP
½ cup icing sugar - sieved
¼ cup butter or margarine
80 gms bitter chocolate (2 slabs of 40 gms each) - Nestle, Amul
¼ cup water
1 egg

1. To prepare the cake, sieve flour, cocoa, soda-bicarb & baking powder together. Keep aside.
2. Beat sugar and eggs with a hand or an electric beater till frothy and the volume becomes nearly four times.
3. Add oil gradually beating the mixture lightly all the time.
4. Gradually add flour while you go on beating the mixture on the lowest speed of the electric beater or very slowly by hand. Do not over beat.
5. Pour into a greased 8" round tin and bake in a preheated oven at 300°F/150°C for 30-40 minutes. Test the cake by inserting a knife or skewer. When it comes out clean remove immediately from the oven.
6. Let the cake cool for 5-10 minutes in the tin before removing from the tin. Remove from the tin & keep aside.

7. Prepare the chocolate icing by beating the butter till smooth & creamy. Sieve the icing sugar and add to the butter. Beat till fluffy. Add sifted cocoa powder gradually, beating after each addition, till you get the desired colour. Add enough cocoa to get a dark, rich chocolate colour. Fill some icing in an icing gun & keep in the lower shelf of the fridge. Chill the left over icing in the freezer for 5-7 minutes.

8. Cut the cake into 3 parts. Spread ½ of the icing on the first piece of cake. Keep the second piece of cake on top. Spread all the icing. Cover with the last piece of cake. Keep in the fridge.

9. To prepare the icing for the top, heat ¼ cup water in a small heavy bottomed pan, with bitter chocolate (broken into small pieces) on low heat, stirring all the time till chocolate dissolves. Add butter and stir.

10. When butter dissolves remove for heat & add sieved icing sugar. Mix till sugar dissolves. Add egg and immediately stir vigorously, otherwise strands will be made. Heat on low fire, stirring continuously till the icing gets a thick smooth pouring consistency. Do not let boil. Immediately pour over the sandwiched cake. Cover sides with a spatula or knife & leave for 2-3 hours for setting.

11. Pipe a border around the cake with the gun.

Nita Mehta's BEST SELLERS

PUNJABI Khaana

BAKES & CAKES
Baking with Confidence!

MICROWAVE
cooking for the Indian kitchen

QUICK
Vegetarian Cooking

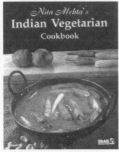

Inadian Vegetarian
Cookbook

Perfect Vegetarian
Cookery

Vegetarian Wonders

Flavours of INDIAN COOKING
(All Colour)
AWARD WINNER

CHINESE
cooking for the Indian kitchen

LOW CALORIE
cooking for the Indian kitchen

PRESSURE COOKING

Vegetarian CURRIES

LOW FAT Tasty Recipes

The best of NON-VEGETARIAN

NAVRATRI Recipes

Indian Low Fat

Eggless OVEN

Mocktails and Snacks

Ice-Creams

Great Ideas- Cooking Tips